Deconstructing

PENGUINS

Deconstructing

PENGUINS

PARENTS, KIDS, AND
THE BOND OF READING

Lawrence and
Nancy Goldstone

BALLANTINE BOOKS

NEW YORK

A Ballantine Book
Published by The Random House Publishing Group

www.ballantinebooks.com

Library of Congress Cataloging-in-Publication Data

Goldstone, Lawrence.
Deconstructing penguins : parents, kids, and the bond of reading / Lawrence and
Nancy Goldstone.— 1st ed.
p. cm.
ISBN 0-8129-7028-4
1. Children—Books and reading.   2. Children's literature—Study and teaching
(Elementary)   3. Reading—Parent participation.   4. Book clubs (Discussion
groups)   I. Goldstone, Nancy Bazelon.   II. Title.
Z1037.A1G597 2005
028.5'5—dc22   2004055440

Printed in the United States of America

2   4   6   8   9   7   5   3   1

First Edition

*For Emily and all the kids
and parents of our book groups*

CONTENTS

Contents

Deconstructing

PENGUINS

CHAPTER 1

PENGUINS 7, JETS 0

How We Got Started

The day we picked to hold our first parent-child book group at our local public library was Sunday, January 10, 1999. Like everything else about the book group, this date and the time—3:30 in the afternoon—had been carefully chosen after months of planning. The first Sunday in January seemed ideal because, as the school vacation had just ended, families would be home and the children would be refreshed. We chose late afternoon to minimize potential conflicts with the other myriad activities in which Connecticut second graders participate. We knew, for example, that the basketball league held its games on Saturday, ice-skating lessons were Sunday morning, the Sunday dance rehearsals for the *Nutcracker* were over, and soccer practice wouldn't resume until early April.

It turned out, however, that we hadn't thought of everything. The hapless New York Jets, a team that had not made the NFL play-offs in eight seasons or finished with a good enough record to host a play-off game in two decades, had that year miraculously achieved both. The young and hungry Jacksonville Jaguars were coming to town on, when else, January 10, and the winner would then meet the Denver Broncos for the right to go on to the Super Bowl.

Interest in the game approached the fanatical. The Meadowlands drew the second-largest crowd in the history of the stadium. (The largest had been for the pope.) Kickoff was set for one P.M., which put the start of our little book group somewhere in the middle of the fourth quarter, when every living creature in the New York metropolitan area would be frozen in front of a television set.

At the last minute, however, it appeared that the fates might yet be with us. The game had descended into a rout and the Jets held a 31–14 lead at the beginning of the fourth quarter. By the time we piled into the car to head for the children's department of the library with our books, markers, large writing pad, and enough cookies and juice to ensure the loyalty of our audience, we had brightened substantially. "No one needs to stay and see the end of *that*," we said.

But no sooner had we backed out of the driveway—with the radio tuned to the game, of course—then Jacksonville scored a touchdown. During the five-minute trip to the library, they scored again. Before we could unload the car, the Jets had been intercepted and the potent Jacksonville offense had the ball once more.

"Hang on to your hats," trumpeted the announcer. "This is gonna be a wild finish."

With indefatigable if slightly forced good cheer, we

trudged in and dragged our paraphernalia up the stairs to the meeting room. We set up an easel for the pad at the front of the room, laid out the snacks, and waited. Ten minutes later, we were still the only people in the room.

Finally, the door opened and a librarian stuck her head in. "Someone named Katherine's mother called to say that they can't make it this time but they'll be here next time, and one of the other parents called to say that neither the father nor the son had read the book and did that matter?"

At 3:27, a mother and daughter walked in, looked around at the empty room, and wordlessly sat down. Soon another mother and daughter arrived and then, astoundingly, a father and daughter. They were followed closely by another father and his son. The first father and the second father exchanged a glance, the meaning of which was all too clear. Soon, we had ten second graders, each with a parent, four of whom were distressed fathers. When the last of the fathers entered, he gave the final, damning report.

"Down to a seven-point lead. Still four minutes to go."

The dads all sunk a little lower in their seats, then, as one, turned to face us. We could read "This had better be worth it" written plainly on each of their faces. As they say in comedy . . . a tough room.

And so we launched into the afternoon's offering: *Mr. Popper's Penguins.*

Mr. Popper's Penguins is about a housepainter who lives in a small town called Stillwater. Mr. Popper lives with Mrs. Popper and two little Poppers. He does not make a lot of money, possibly because he is so busy daydreaming about traveling to the Antarctic (a big deal in 1938 when this book was written). He couldn't work in the winter, so he spent his time reading about explorers. As the story opens, he has just sent a letter to Admiral Drake, a famous Antarctic explorer, extolling the virtues of penguins. Admiral Drake responds by sending Mr. Popper a penguin of his very own.

Lots of humorous mishaps occur and a female penguin arrives, which quickly gives rise to ten additional penguins. Mr. Popper, in an attempt to afford all these penguins, takes them on the road as a stage act. They are wildly successful, earning the Poppers lots of money that they spend entirely on the penguins. Eventually, however, Mr. Popper and the penguins land in jail in New York from which they are rescued by Admiral Drake, who has just returned from his expedition. So impressed is Admiral Drake with Mr. Popper that he takes him on his next voyage. The book closes with an illustration of a smiling Mr. Popper in a fur hood, next to a penguin, looking over the railing of a ship.

"Welcome to the book group! Thank you all for coming," we said, after everyone had gone around the room and introduced themselves and we'd made it clear to the kids that we were going to discuss the book for a while *before* we broke for snacks. "Books are like puzzles," we began. "The author's ideas are hidden and it is up to all of us to figure them out. Whenever you read a book you want to know what the book is *really* about, not what it's about on the surface, not the story, but what's underneath the story. . . ."

A little boy's hand went up.

"Yes, Jeremy? Do you have an idea about what the book is really about?"

Jeremy (we've obviously changed all the names) was one of those kids you run into from time to time who appears to be actually a miniature adult. He was dressed in an Oxford shirt, V-neck sweater, corduroys, and what appeared to be little Rockport shoes. He stared intensely for a moment.

"*Mr. Popper's Penguins* is about a man named Mr. Popper," he reported. "Mr. Popper gets a penguin in the mail who he trains. Then he gets another penguin. They have babies. Then they go to New York."

"That's good, Jeremy, but that's the story. We're looking for what the author is trying to say *underneath* the story. What the story is *really* about. What do you think the story is *really* about?"

Jeremy nodded. "They get in trouble in New York. They even go to jail. Admiral Drake gets them out. Then Mr. Popper and the penguins go on the boat with Admiral Drake."

"Yes, Jeremy, that's very good." Oh dear, we thought.

We tried some different, open-ended questions, like "Why do you think the authors chose penguins?" but it was proving impossible to move either the kids or the parents off the plot. After about twenty minutes, our worst fears were being realized: blank stares from the kids, restlessness from the parents, long silences, and two heavily perspiring moderators.

We continued to flounder until we asked, "The town

that Mr. Popper lived in . . . what kind of a place was it? Why do you think the authors chose the name Stillwater? Was it just an accident?"

This had more success. One little girl said that she didn't think it was an accident and we quickly (and gratefully) moved into a discussion of Stillwater. Everyone in the town except Mr. Popper, the kids quickly noticed, was "dull." They were "boring," "ordinary," and "did what everyone else did." "What do you think about people like that?" we asked. "How would you describe them in one word?"

Rebecca, a girl in the back, waved her hand furiously. "NORMAL," she replied with triumph. The parents chuckled but shifted uneasily in their seats.

"What about Mr. Popper?" we went on. He was certainly not normal, the kids agreed. He was . . . they couldn't seem to find the right word. So, on the easel, we wrote:

D _ _ _ _ _ _ _ _

A mother raised her hand. "Demented?" she offered.

"Nooooo."

"Dumb?" suggested one of the little boys, obviously not a spelling whiz.

"Noooo."

"What about 'different'?" asked another mother.

"Yes! And what made him different?"

After a little more discussion it came out. Mr. Popper was different because he had a dream, and he was the only one in the town who did. What's more, he had done something about it. He had followed his dream.

"Could this be a book about the importance of following your dreams?" we asked. "Was that what the book was *really* about?"

There was a slow nodding of heads.

"So," we went on, "what did everyone think of this? Was it good to follow your dreams, or even to keep them?" The expression on each parent's face changed. We went around the room, first asking each child, then each parent, "What is your dream?"

The kids, of course, had no trouble with this question. Although a couple had the very suburban dream of making a million dollars, there were also dreams of travel, adventure, and even world peace. When we came to Annabeth, a thoroughly adorable, cherubic little blond girl, she had no problem at all.

"My dream is that my brother gets eaten by a bear," she said happily.

For the parents, however, the question proved enormously difficult. One mother refused to answer at all. Another said that she had no dreams because her life was perfect. A couple of parents tried to get around the question with bad jokes. A few, however, tried to be honest. A mother said that she had always dreamed of making a documentary film and a father dreamed that he had never given up chemistry for law. One father was particularly pensive. We knew him from the weekend soccer league. He was an intense marketing executive who appeared to have been chiseled out of brick. "I always dreamed I could fly," he said softly, leaving no doubt that he wasn't referring to airplanes.

We went on to discuss why it was important to have

dreams. The parents, many of whom had clearly just been reminded that they had ever had dreams at all, were particularly insistent that their kids hang on to theirs. We spent some time discussing what it takes to be able to hang on to a dream.

Then we went back to the subject of being different—not just the *act* of being different but the willingness to be different. It didn't seem to have bothered Mr. Popper in the least that he was different. This, of course, is a crucial point to get across to kids who are just beginning to face the pressures of social conformity and ostracism—wear the kind of clothes the other kids wear or pay the price. It can be very reassuring to kids to be reminded that being different isn't something that needs to be hidden.

Suddenly the librarian stuck her head into the room and announced that it was five P.M. and the library was closing so we had to leave. When we adjourned, there was applause—it stunned us—and many parents stopped on the way out to say thank you.

Virtue was even rewarded. Jacksonville did not score again and the Jets added an insurance field goal to win by ten points. As a result, everyone got to see them lose the following week in Denver.

When we were asked by our library's friends association to help set up some new programs for the children's department, parent-child book groups seemed an obvious choice.

The growth in book groups had been a phenomenon. Once a month, in cities and towns across America, enthusiastic readers of every stripe were gathering in groups to discuss books. In our own town, almost every adult we knew, including our internist, her father (a gastroenterologist), and her mother (a hard-boiled lawyer) spent an evening every few weeks or so dissecting a novel that none of them would ever have found the time to read without the incentive of a book group meeting. Some, like our doctor's family, paid a trained moderator to lead the discussion and pick the books; others searched Web sites and culled through reviews for material. Our library had even hired someone from Chicago specifically to establish an adult book group program.

It seemed only natural to extend this concept to include children. A parent-child reading group would be an opportunity for parents to actually *do* something with their kids instead of trying to squeeze in a few hours of "quality time" in between ferrying them back and forth from soccer games or swim meets. Also, we knew from discussions with our friends that many were having an extraordinarily difficult time getting their kids to resist the seductive lure of television or the computer screen in order to pick up a book. Anxious parents were e-mailing children's reading lists back and forth, trying to find some key to getting their kids to read. And the problem was not restricted to our town. Judging from the number of articles that appeared in newspapers and magazines, parental concern about reading proficiency cut across geographic, economic, racial, and political lines.

We decided to aim at elementary school children, specifically at grades two through four, mostly because our daughter was in the second grade and we felt that she and her friends would benefit from a book discussion. Having no experience with this sort of thing, we thought a little research might be in order, so we started making appointments with the reading resource teachers and librarians at each of the local elementary schools. We wanted to get a sense of what their approach to reading was, and also to get some suggestions for our reading list.

We were told much the same thing by every teacher and librarian with whom we spoke. They said that reading was very important, that children wanted to talk about the books they read, that a parent-child book group was a good idea, but that we shouldn't make it too hard. Children are easily discouraged, they insisted. If they don't understand some of the words, they'll put the book down. Give them books they're familiar with, books with simple language, an entertaining style, and an obvious message. A little bathroom humor wouldn't hurt either. It doesn't matter what they read as long as they read *something,* they said. Some of the reading resource teachers suggested books that played off pop culture, like *Goosebumps,* or thumbnail biographies of people like Shaquille O'Neal or Tiger Woods.

The only person who disagreed with this philosophy was the woman in charge of the reading program for the entire elementary school system. Reading was becoming a lost art, she said, and she personally wished the language arts curriculum was stronger. But the curriculum came from the local board of education and the state requirements, and she was not able to change it.

We left these meetings confused, and not a little disturbed. We were convinced that it mattered a great deal what a child read. We viewed children's pop fiction like adult pop fiction—for entertainment only. There were no greater issues, no underlying themes, nothing to prompt critical thought. A child's eyes could simply slide over the words—a kind of literary candy. We couldn't use these books for a book group; there was nothing there to discuss.

Also, we felt that restricting children to that type of book denied them the excitement of discovering the beauty of language and the passion and power of meaningful ideas. The real danger of turning kids off from reading and hurling them permanently in the direction of electronic media, we were convinced, was in making the books too superficial. Whatever had happened, we wondered, to breaking a book down by its various elements—plot, character, conflict—in order to decipher its themes, to working at revealing the author's design and then assessing its implications?

There was one other aspect to the make-it-easy method that we found particularly troubling. We were told that one of the principal reasons that the state had adopted this approach to reading was that children in inner-city and lower-income schools were not capable of handling anything deeper or more sophisticated. In addition to finding this position insulting, we felt that there was no group more in need of critical reading skills than those very children. At age seven, there is not that much difference in children's curiosity or learning ability, and so structuring a curriculum to incorporate real discussion would not be all that difficult. It seemed to us that the people who were un-willing to take on a little challenge were not the kids but the policy-making educators.

So, despite everything we had been told, we decided to try our own ideas. Of course, having an idea is one thing, making it work is something else again.

CHAPTER 2

EVERYONE LOVES A MYSTERY

Learning to Be a Book Detective

It wasn't until after that first discussion of *Mr. Popper's Penguins* that we realized that simply assigning a more complex, layered book wasn't going to be enough to spark a lively, penetrating debate among seven- and eight-year-olds and their parents. The notion that in a good book—any good book, adult or children's—there was something going on under the story that the author was trying to communicate through the characters and the plot was apparently a revelation, and not just to the kids. ("Do all books have hidden meanings?" a father in one of our later fourth-grade groups asked incredulously after a discussion of *Call of the Wild*.) If those first twenty minutes of fumbling taught us anything, it was that we were going to need a plan.

So, for self-preservation as much as anything else, we tried to rough out a technique that would work more or less with every book. Our approach not only had to reveal layers of truth, we decided, but each layer had to spark interest in reaching the next. We didn't want just a series of questions in a specific order—what do you do if one doesn't work and the rest are dependent on it? We were looking for a framework within which discussion could go on as long as the participants had anything meaningful to say.

It was while we were kicking around this idea of how to get below the surface and still keep everybody's attention that it finally occurred to us that every work of fiction is actually a mystery. After all, you don't know what is going to happen until the end. Will Charlotte save Wilbur? Will Claudia find out if the statue in the Metropolitan Museum of Art is really a Michelangelo? Will Buck finally go free in the wild? All of these are mysteries. The desire to find out is what keeps the reader turning the pages. How much or how little you want to find out is dependent on the author's dexterity in creating characters, setting stakes, and manipulating the story. A skilled writer will lay out this mystery like a trail of bread crumbs—visible enough to keep the reader following along, but not so visible as to make it too easy.

The All-Fiction-Is-Mystery idea turned out to be an especially useful tactic for kids' books because *everyone* loves a mystery. Even more, everyone loves to be the detective who solves the puzzle. When we began to communicate to the kids that in reading a book they were actually entering a crime scene where they were to be responsible for identifying clues, figuring out how the deed was done (method) and why it was done (motive), the discussions suddenly took off. Eventually, we learned to begin all our new second-grade groups with the same question.

"Who knows what a genre is?"

Occasionally we get a seven- or eight-year-old who knows the answer, but usually it's a parent who will reply, "A kind of a category."

"Right. Actually genre comes from French and means a style or type, in this case of books. Can you list some genres for us?"

The kids like this. We usually get science fiction first, followed closely by fantasy, historical fiction, horror, gross books, mystery, sports books, romance (this from a mom), biography, spy fiction, technothrillers (from a dad), and so on.

We list them all and then say, "Very good, but we disagree. We think there is only one genre in fiction. Can anyone guess what that is?"

We inevitably get a lot of blank stares, followed by some tentative hand-raising.

"Chapter books?" a kid will hazard. (Parents will look hopeful at this.)

After a lot of similar guesses, sooner or later, by process of elimination, a boy or girl will raise his or her hand and say, "Mystery?"

"Right! Because," we say, "you don't know what is going to happen until you finish the book. But what happens in the story is just the mystery on the surface. There's another, much more important mystery to solve. It's hidden in the story, and the clues are in the plot, the setting, the makeup of the characters, the interaction between them, and the resolution. It's your job to figure out what the author is really trying to say. When you do, you'll know what the book is about.

"To do this," we tell the kids, "you will have to learn to become book detectives. You'll have to figure out who the suspects are—the characters—analyze their behavior for clues, come up with potential solutions, rule out false leads, and then solve the case."

To extend this metaphor, that first year, we tried to work Sherlock Holmes into the discussion. (It's not by accident, after all, that Sherlock Holmes is the number one all-time best-selling character in fiction.) We obviously couldn't do an actual Conan Doyle story in the second grade, but we did find *Basil of Baker Street* (now unfortunately out of print), a tale in which a mouse named Basil, who lives in the detective's famous flat, solves crimes using the Holmesian method of deductive reasoning.

We were perhaps a bit overzealous in our eagerness to draw the parallel. At the beginning of the hour, when we were discussing setting and Basil's living quarters, a father raised his hand and said, "It's the most famous address in fiction—221 Baker Street."

"221B Baker Street," we blurted out, unable to stop ourselves from correcting him.

Another father turned to him with a grin. "Partial credit," he said.

We continued to tinker around, but we knew that, ultimately, we needed to find some way to provide everyone in the room with the skills necessary to remove each layer of plot, character, and setting until they reached the core. We finally found the answer by examining the process of writing a novel and then working backwards. Having written fiction ourselves, we understood that there were definite steps that almost every writer goes through in order to produce a finished work.

The first thing an author usually does is to decide what he or she wants to write about. This will create the underlying theme of the book. For example, an author may decide to examine the concept of loyalty, or discuss the nature of real courage. Others may choose an underlying theme with political connotations or simply how to deal with personal challenges such as divorce or peer pressure.

Once an author has decided what to write about, he or she must then choose a plot, characters, and setting to best convey that message to the reader. An author choosing to write about courage, for example, may opt for a story as dramatic as Gary Paulsen's *Hatchet,* where a child is left alone (plot) in the woods (setting) to fend for himself, or one as seemingly tame as *The View from Saturday* by E. L. Konigsburg, which simply places a child who is different (plot) in the midst of a perfectly normal American middle school (setting). Some authors, like Dick King-Smith or E. B. White, choose to populate their stories with animals instead of people, while Madeline L'Engle opts for the cosmos as her setting.

Next come specific characters. (Obviously, not everyone works this way or follows a checklist, but all writers have to deal with these elements in some fashion along the way.) Generally, particularly in children's literature, the author will choose one character to embody the underlying theme. But in order to create the sort of tension and conflict that makes any novel work, the author will also create a second character with an opposing point of view or set of values from the first. Identifying and understanding these two characters—they are called the protagonist and antagonist—is vital to revealing the underlying theme.

Most novelists don't know every detail, plot twist, or side character when they first sit down to write. As the book progresses, they begin to flesh out the story with an off-center character here or a false trail there, all to make the reader's journey richer and more entertaining. But even here, there can be clues to an author's overall intention. Nothing makes it into a novel by accident. Everything is there by conscious choice. Twists and turns are often inserted not just for suspense but to highlight some issue or conflict in the story.

But be careful! It is against the rules for a book detective—or any detective—to manufacture evidence. That means that unless a theory is specifically supported in the text by a passage, a character, a description, or a chain of events, it is not admissible. Just like a real detective cannot assert "I have no evidence but I'm sure the accused must have done this," a book detective cannot say "There's nothing in the book, but I'm sure the author must have meant this."

So now we tell our young sleuths and their parents to stick to the hard evidence and go first to the essentials—protagonist and antagonist, setting, plot, and conflict. In most novels, the author has worked very carefully to weave all of these elements into the story, so these clues are the most revealing. When they were finished sifting and evaluating the data, we told our groups, they could work their way right back into the author's mind.

Even using all the evidence properly, however, there can sometimes be more than one theory of a crime. Book interpretations are subjective. After all, no one was actually sitting in the room with the author. The only rule is that an interpretation must be consistent with the facts. A group may come up with two perfectly logical but utterly incompatible theories as to what the book is really about. This is not a weakness but a strength. The discussion by the proponents on either side enlarges the perspective of everyone in the room. After all, what is a better lesson for kids (and adults) than to learn that other people may see things differently and still make sense?

And there need be no ultimate resolution of the disagreement. There is great value in agreeing to disagree. We have one father and daughter—the girl is Rebecca, the one who proclaimed "Normal" in *Mr. Popper's Penguins*—who have been with us since the very beginning. Rebecca is now going into the eighth grade. Her father, a lawyer, has been invaluable to our groups as he always (and we mean *always*) comes up with a different interpretation of the book than anyone else. He is unfailingly generous and good-natured, even when his odd perspective is greeted with mock groans by his compatriots, but nonetheless refuses to back down.

Just last year he again arrived at one of his unique solutions, and claimed that he and Rebecca had discussed this at length and Rebecca had agreed. At that, he crossed his arms and sat back in his chair with great satisfaction.

"But I didn't agree," said Rebecca.

"Yes, you did," her dad insisted. "Why are you changing your mind now?"

"Because we're always *wrong*!" Rebecca cried.

"So what?" he retorted. "We may be wrong, but we're always interesting."

Even after we had completed the what-is-this-book-really-about stage, our approach still felt incomplete. We wanted the kids to learn not just to retrace an author's steps, but also to evaluate the message and how it was presented. After all, there are rules to writing fiction as well. Authors must stay consistent within the world they have created. They can't cheat the reader (however tempting). Changes in character have to be explained, and no character should act against his or her basic nature for the author's convenience. Settings, even in fantasy books, should have an underlying truth and contribute honestly to the overall story line. Resolutions should evolve naturally and honestly from character traits and plot situations that have already been established. It is just as important to decide if a message has been presented fairly as knowing what the message is.

So, following the mystery metaphor, we decided to go

from the crime scene to the courtroom. (Everyone loves a good trial, too.) After a group comes to an agreement as to a book's underlying message—or agrees to disagree—we ask some final questions. Did the author play fair? Did he or she throw in a character or plot twist that didn't fit the facts? Did the characters act honestly? Were they too one-sided? Did the ending seem faked somehow? Did the author seem to understand what he or she was actually saying, or did the message seem to be different from what the author intended?

From the first, both the kids and their parents loved this part. The idea that they could question the implicit authority that a book and its author carry was irresistible. Even the younger children proved capable of spotting contrivances and shortcuts.

The kids and parents also saw how a judgment on whether or not an author followed the rules could be based on individual point of view. Once, during a discussion of *Animal Farm,* Leslie, an intense fourth grader whose family, we knew, were ferocious environmentalists and animal rights advocates, said that George Orwell's ending was "completely bogus."

"Why?" we asked. "What part of the ending?"

"The part where the pigs ate so much that they got double chins. Pigs would never really do that. He wasn't being fair to pigs."

It was something of a shock—and a great relief—to find out that the "book detective" method actually worked. Once the parents and kids had the general idea, everyone had a lot of fun figuring out what the book was really about, and the eight-year-olds turned out to be surprisingly adept at ferreting out a book's protagonist and antagonist. This in turn made it a whole lot easier for the moderators, which, let's face it, was one of our goals. At this point, many of our groups seem almost to run themselves.

CHAPTER 3

THE GIFT OF THE GREEKS

Protagonist, Antagonist, and the Use of Character

The first step in the book detective method is explaining the concept of protagonist and antagonist to the group. When we began, we realized that even parents didn't really understand either term.

"What is a protagonist?" we asked.

"The hero," said one parent.

"The good guy," said a kid.

"The main character," offered another parent.

"Not exactly," we said. "Actually, protagonist and antagonist originated in the ancient Greek theater. Any of you kids know when ancient Greece was?"

Not a hand.

"Okay, take a guess. Was it before or after the dinosaurs?"

"After."

"Good. Was it before or after your grandparents were born?"

"Before."

"Right. So ancient Greece was some time between the dinosaurs and your grandparents."

The ancient Greeks thought theater was very important, we tell them, and made a big deal about plays. In each play, the *protagonist* was the character in the story who was trying to push the action forward, and the *antagonist* was the character in the story who was trying to hold the action back. When one person is pushing forward and the other is holding back, there is conflict. If you can determine which character is the protagonist and which is the antagonist, and what the conflict is about, you will have come a long way toward figuring out what the story is about.

We knew that to explain these concepts to an elementary school child, we would have to make them personal. So we generally have the following conversation.

"Tommy"—picking a child at random—"do you have a bedtime? A time when you are supposed to go to bed at night?"

Since Tommy is in the seven- to eight-year-old range, this is likely to be a correct supposition.

"Okay, Tommy, we're going to go out on a big limb here, but we bet there are times when you want to stay up later than your bedtime. Is that right?"

It almost always turns out that this *is* right.

"Tell us, have you ever employed strategies for staying up late? For example, 'I'm hungry,' 'I'm thirsty,' 'I'm not tired yet,' 'Just wait until I'm done with this'?"

Tommy will, in fact, have employed one or more of these strategies at some time in the recent past.

"So, Tommy, if the action is staying up late and you are the protagonist, pushing the action forward, who is the antagonist holding the action back? Who is it that tries to stop you from staying up late at night? Who says 'no snack,' 'no drink,' 'I don't care if you're not tired yet,' 'right now and not a second later'?"

Every kid gets this one. "MOM," says Tommy.

"So that is one example of protagonist and antagonist. Tommy is the protagonist, pushing the action of staying up past his bedtime forward, and Mom is the antagonist, trying to hold the action back. The conflict is about who runs Tommy's life, Tommy or someone else. This, then, is a book about justice and democracy. Let's try another one.

"Eloise, do you have any chores around the house?"

Eloise has to clean her room and make her bed.

"Eloise, do you ever feel like not doing your chores?"

"Sometimes," Eloise admits.

"Is there someone there to remind you to make your bed?"

"Mom."

"If the action is getting you to do your chores, who is pushing the action forward?"

"Mom."

"So that makes Mom the . . ."

"Protagonist," says Eloise.

"And if Mom is the protagonist, who is the antagonist, holding back the action of getting the chores done?"

"Me," says Eloise.

We stress that the protagonist is not necessarily the same thing as the hero. Nor is the antagonist necessarily the villain. A protagonist may turn out to be the detestable character and the antagonist someone who is seemingly benign, even sympathetic. The conflict between them, the action that one is pushing forward and one is holding back, is not necessarily violent or physical. Conflict in a story can be as simple as two ideas butting up against one another.

It will be easier to understand how this works and why it is important if we use some real examples. Let's begin with *Charlotte's Web*.

(In this and all the discussions that follow, we have used real responses from parents and kids, but these are not transcripts—we don't have any transcripts. We did take notes, however, and after doing a book for four or five years, we have also learned to appreciate the value of repetition. In order to make the line of each discussion clear and easy to understand, in some cases we have edited questions and answers from a specific group, and in others used an amalgam of discussions that we've had over the years.)

Charlotte's Web

Charlotte's Web by E. B. White is a classic, which means that many parents will probably remember reading it when they were young. For those who didn't, or need a refresher, it is the story of a young pig named Wilbur, who is saved from an untimely death (he was the runt of the litter) first by an eight-year-old girl named Fern, and later by Charlotte, an extremely impressive spider. Wilbur lives on Homer Zuckerman's farm in a barn with Charlotte, Templeton the rat, geese, chickens, sheep, horses, and ducks.

To save Wilbur from being turned into Christmas dinner, Charlotte, who is Wilbur's only friend, weaves words about him into her web. She writes "Some Pig," and later, "Terrific," "Radiant," and "Humble."

The Zuckermans take this as a miracle and spread it around town, with the result that Wilbur becomes famous. When the Zuckermans take him to the county fair, Wilbur wins a special prize, and his survival is assured. Charlotte dies alone but happy at the fairgrounds—Wilbur having bribed Templeton to help him carry her egg sac back to Zuckerman's barn. In the end, three of Charlotte's children stay in the barn with Wilbur and the legacy of their friendship endures.

Most children love *Charlotte's Web* and are eager to discuss it. The last time we did this with our second graders, we began by asking them to tell us what they thought the book was really about *before* we had the discussion, as a kind of game to see who would be closest after we talked about the book. We got back:

- Friendship and how friends help each other out
- Believing
- Problem solving (a mom)
- The difference written words can make (a mom)
- The circle of life (a mom)
- Eating
- Helping
- Diversity (a dad)
- Taking a chance
- What miracles really are (a mom)
- Enjoying your life

There are two distinct approaches to life articulated in the story, one, as it turns out, is that of the protagonist, the

---

other, that of the antagonist. We asked the group who they thought the protagonist was and got back: Charlotte, Mr. Zuckerman, Wilbur, and Fern.

Charlotte is always the first answer—after all, the book *is* called *Charlotte's Web*. As for the other nominations, there is a tendency to want to give *some* answer. We run into this even in groups for the higher grades. In this case, once Charlotte is taken, there is always a certain floundering to try and find someone else who might fill the bill. We handle this by voting and our groups always vote overwhelmingly for Charlotte. Even the people who nominated the other characters usually vote for her in the end.

Once Charlotte is identified as the protagonist, we move on to the antagonist. Here we usually get: Templeton, Wilbur, Mr. Zuckerman, Fern, and Mrs. Zuckerman.

In this book, the identification of the antagonist is more difficult. (The overlap in nominations for protagonist and antagonist is not unusual. Often, when an important character fails to be elected as protagonist, he or she is immediately assumed to be the antagonist.) When we voted here, Wilbur, Fern, and Mrs. Zuckerman were all eliminated pretty quickly, leaving Templeton and Mr. Zuckerman.

"Maybe," we said, "it will help us figure out what is really going on if we list some of each character's traits. Let's begin with Charlotte. What are her characteristics?"

- She really liked Wilbur.
- She was a good friend.
- Willing to help
- Very cheerful
- Caring
- A mother
- Hairy
- Persistent and committed

- Wise
- Used her life wisely
- A spider
- Smart
- A hard worker
- Knows that people are gullible
- Talented
- Brave

- Died after she laid her eggs
- Determined to save Wilbur
- Never got to see her babies
- Her babies were like her.
- Tried beyond herself
- Practical

With all these traits—and they are all correct—there is often something critical that is missed.

"How does Charlotte get her food?"

"She weaves a web and catches flies in it," said Julie, a brown-eyed girl wearing a sparkly T-shirt, who appeared to only barely resist adding "yuck" to the sentence.

"She drinks their blood," Adam added happily. Adam was still in his soccer uniform and had obviously refused to wash his hands and face after his game.

How does Wilbur feel about this initially? He is appalled and disgusted. He thinks Charlotte is "bloodthirsty."

"What is Charlotte's response?" we asked.

Everyone dove for the book.

"She says that no one brings her food like Mr. Zuckerman feeds Wilbur," said Courtney, who got her hand up first.

"She has to live by her own wits," said her mom.

"What does that mean?"

"She has to be smart."

"She has to think."

This is an extremely important clue. Charlotte is able to come up with a plan for Wilbur because she is used to thinking. Wilbur is not used to thinking. At one point, Wilbur, following the instructions of the goose, breaks out of his pen and gets into the orchard. There is a hullabaloo while Zuckerman and the hired man try to get him back. Wilbur decides that freedom is too scary; he prefers his place in the barn after all.

"So Charlotte is smart and practical, and she thinks. If you had to sum up Charlotte's view of the world and her place in it," we asked, "what would it be?"

"That everybody has the right to survive," said a dad.

"That everybody should help others," added his daughter Samantha.

This is crucial. Charlotte believes that the best way to live is through generosity. This philosophy is at the heart of the book. Once we get there, we move on.

"What are the antagonist's traits?" we asked. "What is Templeton like?"

- Likes food
- Selfish
- Fat
- Doesn't care about anyone except himself
- Doesn't care about Wilbur dying
- He's a rat.
- He won't do something good without getting paid for it.
- No conscience

How do the other animals regard Templeton?
"They hate him," said Joe with relish.

"They are scared of him," said Julie.

"Why?"

"He's selfish."

"He's mean."

"The author says that Templeton wasn't above killing a gosling," said Adam's father. "The geese knew that, and they had to watch him pretty closely."

"Exactly. So what would you say Templeton's philosophy of life is?" we asked.

Samantha's father summed it up nicely. "What's in it for me?" he said.

Okay, so that's Templeton. Our other possibility for antagonist was Mr. Zuckerman. Mr. Zuckerman is Charlotte's antagonist in that he wants to kill Wilbur, certainly an important point. But why does he want to do it? Is he doing it to be mean?

"No," said Brittany. "He wants to eat him. People eat pork."

"How do you feel about that? Is Mr. Zuckerman wrong to eat pigs? Should he stop eating pigs so Wilbur can live?"

"No," Brittany continued uncertainly. "Everybody has to eat something. Charlotte eats flies."

"She drinks their blood," Adam noted once again.

"The point is, is Mr. Zuckerman deliberately cruel to Wilbur? He's not, is he? He's actually rather fond of him, isn't he? He brings him his food, scratches him behind the ears, tells him he's some pig. He's not really mean or uncaring to anyone in the book, is he?"

A few years back when we said this, Heather, a little blond, freckle-faced girl waved her hand wildly. She had

Norman Rockwell eyebrows, the kind that lifted up almost to her hairline. "But Mr. Zuckerman *is* mean," she protested hotly. "He's mean to *Mrs*. Zuckerman."

Mr. Zuckerman mean to Mrs. Zuckerman? They hardly exchange two words in the book. "Where? Find the place," we said.

Heather flipped desperately through her book to page 153. "Here," she said finally.

"Does my hair look all right?" asked Mrs. Zuckerman.
"Looks fine," snapped Mr. Zuckerman . . .
"You didn't even *look* at my hair!" said Mrs. Zuckerman.

"*See!*" said Heather triumphantly.

That objection notwithstanding, the majority of the group will agree that Mr. Zuckerman has no real conflict with Charlotte. He is not Charlotte's antagonist; Templeton is. Charlotte, through her quest to save Wilbur, is pushing forward the idea that it is better to live your life helping others. Templeton is trying to hold that idea back by insisting that survival is based on looking out for number one—that is, the selfish pursuit of one's own best interests.

Who is right? On the surface, it would seem that Templeton's philosophy has reaped substantial rewards. After all, how does he end up?

"He gets to live," said Julie's mom.

"He gets to eat all he wants," agreed Samantha.

"He gets to eat *first*," said Ben, a shy boy who hadn't spoken before. "That's the deal Wilbur made with him.

Templeton brings Charlotte's egg sac back to the barn and he gets to eat out of Wilbur's trough first every time."

"He gets *really* fat," observed Adam with satisfaction.

"And what does Charlotte get?" we asked.

"Charlotte dies," said Courtney.

"Doesn't sound fair, does it?" we said. "But then, what does Charlotte say to Wilbur *before* she dies? Can anyone find her last conversation with him?"

"Charlotte says, 'By helping you, perhaps I was trying to lift up my life a trifle. Heaven knows anyone's life can stand a little of that,' " read Samantha.

"What does that mean?" we asked. "That she was trying to 'lift up her life a trifle'?"

"She was trying to make the best of her life," Ben's mother offered. "She was trying to make a contribution."

"To leave a legacy," another parent agreed.

"She was proud of what she did, she had done something good for Wilbur," said Brittany.

"She sort of gave her life some significance, didn't she?" we asked. "She made her time on earth more profound by giving to someone else. And as a result, she died at peace, and happy. And was she so different from us? After all, she says, 'What's a life, anyway? We're born, we live a little while, we die.' Isn't that true of human beings as well?"

"It's true of everything," said Julie's mom.

"And Templeton, is he happy at the end?"

"Not really," said Samantha's dad.

"Templeton's never happy," said Ben.

"Right," we said. "Templeton has been unhappy, mean,

and miserable his whole life. What does the author say about life? On the basis of this book, how do you think he feels about it?"

In fact, *Charlotte's Web* is one long hymn to the precious beauty of the natural world.

"He loves life," said Courtney's mom. "He loves nature and the changing seasons."

"At the very end, Wilbur decides that the barn is the very best place to be," added Courtney.

Once we identified the basic message, we moved on to the key supporting characters. After all, every character in a book has been created by the author for a reason. In *Charlotte's Web,* we always discuss Fern, the little girl who originally saves Wilbur.

"What was Fern like in the beginning?" we asked.

- ▶ Likes animals
- ▶ Cares about animals
- ▶ Raises Wilbur like he's her baby
- ▶ She's pure.
- ▶ She's innocent.
- ▶ She cares about injustice.

"And what was she like at the end?"

- ▶ Cares about different things
- ▶ Doesn't go to the barn
- ▶ Thinks about Henry Fussy
- ▶ Thinks about the Ferris wheel ride
- ▶ Doesn't care as much about Wilbur and what goes on at the farm

"Fern grows up," said Brittany's mom.

"Yes. The author seems to be saying that when you grow up you put some of your caring for others behind you. Do you think that's necessarily true? Do you think that when you guys grow up you will forget about the things you cared about when you were younger?"

All the kids agreed they wouldn't.

Hmmm.

In *Charlotte's Web,* the identity of both the protagonist and antagonist is relatively straightforward, and therefore coming to the underlying message is straightforward as well. In some books, however, the identity of the protagonist and antagonist is not so obvious, and if the reader doesn't get them right, the theme of the book can seem a little strange. Nowhere is this better illustrated than in *Frindle* by Andrew Clements.

Frindle

Nick Allen is a bright, disaffected fifth grader, who, instead of paying attention to the teacher or his schoolwork, spends most of his time trying to figure out how to get away with things. Nick's boredom with school is revealed through pranks like turning up the classroom thermostat, sprinkling sand all over the floor and then announcing a trip to the South Seas. His particular nemesis is his English teacher, the stern, iron-haired Mrs. Granger. To confound Mrs. Granger, who loves words and understanding where they came from, Nick starts calling an ordinary ballpoint pen a "frindle." Mrs. Granger refuses to acknowledge this word. When Nick persuades his classmates to refer to their pens as "frindles" as well, the battle is on, and soon this war of words escalates to an increasingly public test of wills. Nick is even interviewed by a television news reporter. Who will give in, the joyfully rebellious school kids or the hideously rigid school administration?

Luckily for Nick, Madison Avenue intervenes and Nick's father is approached with a plan to patent the name "Frindle" and sell pens under that logo all over America. The plan succeeds, and Nick becomes rich (although his father keeps this from him until after Nick is in college so that it won't affect his work ethic). Although Nick is initially shaken by the controversy he has sparked, he eventually gets over it and starts paying more attention in school. His next joust with the administration is much more productive; he begins a campaign to improve the appalling lunchtime cuisine in the school cafeteria. By the time he goes to college, the word *frindle* has come into such general use that it even appears in the dictionary. In gratitude, Nick sends Mrs. Granger an engraved gold fountain pen and endows a million-dollar scholarship fund in her name.

With some books, a discussion of who might be the protagonist can lead to spirited debate, but in *Frindle* the answer seems obvious—even more obvious than in *Charlotte's Web*—and everyone quickly agrees that it is Nick. Mrs. Granger seems equally obvious for the antagonist.

Okay, if Nick is the protagonist, what are his character traits?

- Creative
- Mischievous
- Made up a word
- Likes to waste time
- Distracts his teacher
- Clever

- Lazy
- Troublemaker
- Doesn't give up fast
- Doesn't like homework
- Thinks school is boring
- Smart

Nick's rebelliousness is extremely appealing to the kids. They love the fact that he refuses to knuckle under to authority. Parents, on the other hand, while uncomfortable with Nick's attitude, cannot help but admire his ingenuity in creating a successful business out of nothing and making gobs of money.

Still, nobody really likes him. The kids are put off by his superior, smart-alecky manner, and the parents are less than thrilled that he makes all of this money while getting out of his schoolwork. But everyone agrees that it is Nick's naming of the pen and then refusing to be beaten down by Mrs. Granger that makes him the protagonist of the book.

So what about the antagonist?

- *Loves* the dictionary
- Wants to stop Nick from making the word
- Strict
- Wants the kids to learn

- Clever
- Creature of habit
- Dull
- Good teacher
- Loves what she does

Mrs. Granger's nomination as antagonist is buttressed by her manner. There hasn't been a single parent or child who hasn't come up against some teacher whom they considered too strict, overbearing, and unreasonable. What difference does it make what Nick calls his pen? This obsession with strictly correct English stifles creativity, so she's the problem, not Nick. You couldn't have a clearer example of holding back action than mean old Mrs. Granger.

But just what action *is* Mrs. Granger holding back? That answer seems obvious as well. Nick had an idea, he was willing to stick to his idea and make it work against the odds. So Mrs. Granger was holding back entrepreneurial capitalism.

Still, no one is ever really satisfied with this interpretation, since society was no better off simply because a ballpoint pen now had a new name. Nick, after all, didn't really *do* anything. This wasn't like Henry Ford inventing the automobile.

So, we ask, did Nick really deserve his success? Is Andrew Clements saying that it doesn't matter what a person does as long as they make a lot of money at it? If that is in fact what the author is saying, how does the group feel about it?

Invariably, everyone agrees that Nick does not deserve the riches he attains. More than that, by promoting crass commercialism, there is a consensus in the room that *Frindle* is not a very good book.

If the message of *Frindle* is this superficial, it either means that Andrew Clements is a pretty shallow guy, or that everybody missed something and there is probably another interpretation. What if, in this case, the obvious answer is not the right answer? In other words, what if Nick is not the protagonist after all? What other character might it be?

"You mean like Mrs. Granger?" someone is sure to ask.

"All right," we agree. "Let's try Mrs. Granger. Then who is the antagonist?"

Of course, it would have to be Nick. So we try it. If Mrs. Granger is the protagonist and Nick is the antagonist, then what is the action? What would Mrs. Granger be pushing forward that Nick is trying to hold back?

"What is Mrs. Granger actually doing?" we ask.

As soon as you start looking at things from Mrs. Granger's point of view, her character becomes much more sympathetic, no matter what she looks like or how she behaves. Suddenly, everyone remembers that the only reason Nick came up with the word *frindle* was because Mrs. Granger had assigned him to do an extra report on where words came from after Nick had tried to weasel out of a homework assignment. Moreover, he actually learned something from doing that report. In fact, he was thinking about where words came from and how they got into the dictionary when he thought to call a pen a "frindle."

"So what is Mrs. Granger really doing?" we ask.

"Making Nick work?"

"Is that bad? That he has to earn what he gets? That he has to learn? That he has to think?"

No, everyone agrees.

"So what action is Mrs. Granger pushing forward?"

"She's pushing *Nick* forward," said a mom. "She's teaching him."

All of a sudden everyone realizes that *Frindle* is a book

about an extremely clever teacher who sees that a very intelligent and talented student is going off on the wrong track and wasting his ability. By forcing him to live through all the consequences of one of his pranks, Mrs. Granger teaches Nick that it *does* matter how you apply your energies. Many years later, after a string of successes, Nick himself realizes what Mrs. Granger did for him back in the fifth grade, and that is why he sends her the fountain pen and endows the scholarship.

CHAPTER 4

LOCATION, LOCATION, LOCATION

The Importance of Setting

A good book detective should always examine the setting—the scene of the crime—for potential clues as to what the book is really about. Getting used to noticing and discussing setting comes in very handy as children are exposed to more advanced literature in middle and upper school. For example, when the Pulitzer Prize–winning playwright Arthur Miller wanted to discuss McCarthyism in the 1950s, he drew parallels between the past and present by setting *The Crucible* during the Salem witch trials. Similarly, H. G. Wells set much of *The Time Machine* in a bleak, distant future in order to comment on class relations in nineteenth-century Britain.

Most children's books employ one of two types of settings, realism or fantasy. In the first case, the author chooses what seems to be a genuine town or community, either in the present or past. There are both limitations and advantages to this approach. It is obviously easier not to have to spend time creating a rationale for a made-up world. On the other hand, with realism, characters have to behave the way actual people do. That can prove unwieldy in a children's book where the themes are usually kept intentionally straightforward.

That is why many authors opt to construct a fantasy world. Fantasy settings allow the author to portray events that might otherwise be disturbing or difficult for children. Most children are capable of keeping distance as long as the world is clearly not their own. Another advantage of a made-up society is that it allows the author to focus on specific traits, emotions, or cultural phenomena without having to worry about real-world concerns. Setting in these books is generally (though not always) intentionally narrow—small isolated communities where reaction to events can be measured and explained simply. But fantasy has its limitations as well. There has to be coherence and logic to even a made-up world, otherwise the setting—and therefore the story—will come across as phony.

One book in which a fantasy setting is beautifully handled is *Babe: The Gallant Pig* by Dick King-Smith. *Babe* is an excellent vehicle for demonstrating the importance of setting to young children. We use it in our second-grade group.

Babe: The Gallant Pig

Babe is the story of a pig that is raffled off at a county fair and ends up with Farmer Hogget and his wife. As those who have seen the film know, the Hoggets run a sheep farm populated by animals who speak to each other but not to the Hoggets. Mrs. Hogget's idea is for Babe to be the centerpiece of a festive Hogget dinner, thereby adding menace right from the start. (This is not too different from the fate originally intended for Wilbur in *Charlotte's Web*. Why pigs, as opposed to, say, cows, are singled out for this treatment in children's books is unclear.)

At the farm, Babe, who is the only pig on the place, is befriended by Fly, the Hogget's sheepdog. Fly is herself the mother of puppies and, feeling sorry for the little orphan pig, she takes him under her paw. (Unlike the film, there is no deaf, crabby father sheepdog, nor is there a miscreant duck, or evil preening cat.) Eventually, Babe, who does not know Mrs. Hogget's grim plans for his future, decides that he wants to herd sheep like his foster mother Fly. He develops his own way of doing it, which not only saves him from the Hoggets' dinner table, but also makes him a star.

"Okay, who can tell us what the setting of this book is?" we always begin.

This is an easy one for children.

"The Hogget farm," said Ryan, red-haired and freckle-faced, who looked like he had just walked off a farm himself.

"Right. Where, exactly, is the Hogget farm?"

This is harder. The author never says where the farm is.

"Well, is it in America, do you think?"

"I don't think so," Claudia answered tentatively, swinging her ponytail.

"Why not?"

"They use funny words," Claudia said. "They say things like 'Blimey.' They call television the 'telly.' "

"Exactly. So this farm is probably somewhere in England, or maybe even Australia or New Zealand. Does it seem to be a big farm, employing a lot of people, or a little farm?"

Everyone agreed it was a little farm, since Farmer and Mrs. Hogget were the only two humans on the place. They also agreed that it was out in the middle of nowhere, not near any big cities.

"*When* is it set, do you think? A long time ago or now?"

Again, there was agreement that the presence of a Land Rover and television, but not cell phones or computers, indicated that the story was intended to take place pretty close to today or at the very least in the not-so-distant past.

"So, what we've got here is an isolated farm, where the outside world does not intrude very often. There are almost no people, only animals. The animals have their own society. It is a closed society, kind of a little world unto itself, isn't it? Why do you think an author would do this?"

"He likes animals?" Ryan's mother replied.

"Maybe. Could there be another reason?"

Eventually someone got around to saying that it helped the author tell his story.

"Has anyone ever heard the term *microcosm*?" we asked. "It comes from the Greek word *mikros*, meaning small, and *cosmos,* meaning world. Put them together, and you get 'little world.' In this case, 'little world' doesn't mean a planet the size of a marble. It means a very small society that is created as an example of a larger world. Your family might be a microcosm of your town. Your class can be a microcosm of second grade. If you wanted to write a story about life in the second grade, you could set it in your classroom and people would understand that you were talking about issues that affect the whole second grade, and maybe even the whole school if your class was representative enough.

"Of course, we're talking about animals in *Babe,* but they are animals who behave like people. So what could the Hogget farm be a microcosm of? Or, let's put it this way: Can what happens on this little sheep farm in the middle of nowhere have anything to do with your life here in this town? Who thinks that what happens on the Hoggets' farm cannot possibly have anything to do with us here today? Raise your hands."

Almost every child raised his or her hand.

"Who thinks it is possible that what happens in this little world *does* have something to do with us today?"

Almost every parent raised his or her hand (plus those children savvy enough to now vote with the adults).

"Okay," we said. "Let's investigate."

We started, once again, with protagonist and antagonist. The kids pretty much recognized that Babe was the protagonist, although some thought it might be Fly, Mr. Hogget, Mrs. Hogget, or even Ma, the ewe. We voted, and Babe won in a landslide.

The next step would ordinarily have been to take nominations for antagonist, but experience has taught us that in this book the antagonist can be difficult for children to identify. Instead, we asked for a list of Babe's characteristics and looked for a character with an opposing set of traits.

- Has adventures
- He's a sheep pig.
- Brave
- Talks to Ma
- Polite

- Curious
- Determined
- Tries to tell Fly that the sheep are not stupid
- Wants to be a sheep pig

In fact, the most important thing about Babe was not on the list. What *is* Babe? He's a *pig*! What's so important about that? Well, how many pigs are there on the Hoggett farm? Just one, and he's an outsider; he has no history with dogs or sheep or people. By putting only one pig into this closed society, King-Smith can reveal the dynamic of the farm and its effect on this different newcomer. Children can also see very clearly Babe's effect on everyone else.

"Has there ever been a pig on the Hogget farm before?" we asked.

Everyone agreed that despite the farmer's surname, Babe was the first pig to live on the Hogget farm.

"How do we know?"

"Fly's puppies don't know what he is," said Elizabeth, her eyes very blue behind her glasses. "They have to ask Fly. She tells them he's a pig."

"Does Fly say anything else to her puppies about Babe?"

"She says Farmer Hogget will eat him when he gets big enough," volunteered David.

"What do the puppies say about that?"

"They ask if Farmer Hogget is going to eat them, too, when they get big enough," answered Matthew, who was sitting next to David and poking him when he wasn't speaking.

"What is Fly's response?"

"She says no, the Hoggets only eat stupid animals like sheep and cows, not clever ones like dogs," said Matthew's mom, glancing over to see what her son was up to.

"Then her puppies ask if pigs are stupid, don't they? Can anyone read what the author says right after that?"

Elizabeth read:

Fly hesitated. On the one hand, having been born and brought up in sheep country, she had in fact never been personally acquainted with a pig. On the other, like most mothers, she did not wish to appear ignorant before her children.

"Yes," she said. "They're stupid."

"How can Fly know that pigs are stupid if she's never met one?" we asked.

"She can't," said Claudia's mom.

"There is a word that describes Fly's action here—the making of a judgment in the absence of information. Does anyone know it?"

Nobody did.

"Why don't we play hangman to see if we can figure it out?"

This suggestion always meets with approval. Children,

especially second and third graders, love hangman. So we wrote:

＿ ＿ ＿ ＿ ＿ ＿ ＿ ＿ ＿ and eventually everyone figured out that the word was *prejudice*.

"Is this a reasonable approach to someone's being different?" we asked. "If someone comes into school with different-colored skin, or speaking a different language, or even wearing different kinds of clothes, should you make a judgment about them based just upon their appearance?"

Fly's words have an even deeper meaning, though, because she says them to her children. "Could the author be trying to say that this is the way prejudice is passed on from generation to generation?" we asked. "Even by a careless word? Because it *was* careless. She regrets it almost immediately, doesn't she?"

"Yes," said Claudia. "She knows Babe isn't stupid."

"But she never tells her puppies, does she? They leave the farm thinking pigs are stupid."

Everyone agreed it is likely that Fly's children will spend their whole lives believing pigs are stupid, and may pass that false information down to *their* children.

"It's kind of a cycle of prejudice, isn't it?" we asked. "Maybe this is a clue to what the book is about. Let's move on to the antagonist and see."

When we asked for possible antagonists, we got Fly, the sheep, and Mrs. Hogget. Mrs. Hogget was eliminated pretty quickly, because even though she initially wanted to cook Babe for Christmas dinner, she became his staunchest supporter after Babe saved the Hoggets' sheep from rustlers. As for the sheep, there's no conflict at all—they just follow Babe's lead, so they can't be the antagonist. That leaves Fly:

- A sheepdog
- Controls the sheep
- Is a mom
- Not polite to the sheep
- Tries to make Babe believe the sheep are stupid

- Black and white
- Bossy
- Loving to Babe
- Friendly to Babe

This is a good time to remind everyone that the antagonist in a story is not necessarily a villain. After all, Fly becomes Babe's foster mother, soothing him when he is lonely and treating him like one of her own puppies. She's proud of him. She's kind and caring. In fact, she loves him. These are all admirable qualities. How then can she be the antagonist?

Well, she doesn't want him to be a sheep pig, someone pointed out. But that's not true. She encouraged him to be a sheep pig. He couldn't have done it without her. But they did clash on one important point. What is that?

The sheep.

Babe, the protagonist, was convinced that sheep were not stupid and should be treated with dignity. The character who was holding that idea back was Fly. This wasn't a case of making a judgment in the absence of experience. Fly had plenty of experience with sheep. She saw them every day. But she had never taken the time or trouble to understand them. Fly had been bred to think she was superior to the sheep and that she needn't be polite to them. They wouldn't understand or respond to politeness anyway.

But Babe, the outsider, was curious, and decided to find out for himself. He spoke politely to Ma and found her both receptive and lucid. Babe tried to convince Fly that the sheep weren't stupid, but Fly wouldn't listen to him. It took a crisis for Fly to come around.

A crisis—or climax—is that part of a book to which everything is building, and after which events become inevitable. There is usually only one climax in a book. It does not take place at the end, as most people believe, but often somewhere in the middle.

When we asked the group where they thought the climax occurred, most of them brought up the chapter called "Oh, Ma!" where two wild dogs threatened the flock. Ultimately, Babe drove the wild dogs away and saved the sheep, but not before the dogs killed Ma. Grief-stricken, Babe tried to lick the blood away from Ma's wounds. Seeing the blood on Babe's snout, Farmer Hogget assumed that it was Babe who had killed Ma. He was about to shoot Babe when Mrs. Hogget yelled to him that the police had telephoned about wild dogs in the neighborhood. It was only then that he realized that, far from killing a sheep, Babe had saved his flock.

But Fly, who was still in the fields, did not know this, and she was frantic. She knew that Farmer Hogget intended to kill Babe and she could not believe that Babe had murdered Ma. She tried to order the sheep to tell her what had really happened, but her aggressive manner only made them more upset and incoherent. In order to find out, Fly was forced to do something she had sworn never to do: treat the sheep with politeness. She had to say, "Please, could you be kind enough to tell me what happened this morning?"

This then is the climax of *Babe*—not violence, not death, but the simple act of saying "please." It worked, and the sheep told Fly what she most wanted to hear—that Babe saved them from the wild dogs. After a lifetime of herding, it was Fly's first real communication with the sheep, and with their response, her antagonism melted away. With the entire farm now cooperating, Babe's success at the sheepdog competition, which ends the book, was assured. He overcame his real adversary—ingrained prejudice—through curiosity, persistence, and politeness.

Not a bad lesson for grade school.

In *Babe,* Dick King-Smith used the controlled setting of a small farm to demonstrate both how prejudice gets started and how it is conquered. The setting and characters also gave some distinct clues as to how the book was going to turn out. The deliberately comic nature of many of the events on the Hogget farm (just the name Hogget is a hint) suggests that, despite various obstacles or even a tragedy, the book will end well.

The famed film director Alfred Hitchcock once said, "You cannot promise and then not deliver." By this, he did not mean that if the audience sees a gun emerge from behind a curtain, that it must go off and someone has to be shot. He simply meant that by introducing the gun, you've established a mood of suspense that must be accounted for. In our groups, we often use "Hitchcock's Law" to determine whether an author has played fair with the reader. In *Babe,* the mood introduced by a pig who wants to herd sheep as well as sheep who sound like the charwomen in *Mary Poppins* satisfies Hitchcock's Law. It would have been out of place to turn Babe into bacon.

But setting can be used to set an ominous mood as well. Another book, this one with a realistic setting, has essentially the same theme as *Babe*—prejudice—but handles the material in a very different way. *White Lilacs* by Carolyn Meyer is intended for an older audience—we do it in fourth grade—but it can be analyzed along similar lines.

White Lilacs

Based on a true incident, *White Lilacs* is set in the small town of Dillon, Texas, in 1921 (the real town was Denton). It is the story of a thriving African-American community, which the residents call Freedomtown, who are threatened with eviction in order to make room for a whites-only city park. The main character is twelve-year-old Rose Lee Jefferson, an aspiring artist, who narrates the events as they unfold. Rose Lee, the first resident of Freedomtown to find out about the whites' scheme, overhears a discussion while she is standing in for her cousin and serving at a dinner party at the home of the wealthy, spoiled Bell family. So unaware are the guests at this dinner party that black people exist that they speak openly in front of Rose Lee and the other servants as if they weren't there.

The book revolves around the way the various members of Freedomtown deal with the crisis. The residents' reactions range from acquiescence to anger, frustration to militancy. These varying points of view are represented by different characters. The owner of the funeral home, for example, one of the wealthiest members of Freedomtown, simply packs up and relocates. Most of the residents, however, do not have that option. Since they are going to get almost nothing from the town for their homes, they will be forced to either move to a filthy, swamp-ridden area called "the Flats," or start over someplace else with nothing.

Then there are those who wish to fight back. These include Henry, Rose Lee's brother, a follower of Marcus Garvey's Back-to-Africa movement, who is eventually tarred and feathered by the Bells' son and his friends for refusing to wash their car, and Rose Lee's aunt Susannah, a light-skinned schoolteacher from St. Louis, who happens to be visiting when the disaster hits.

The key relationship is between Rose Lee and the Bells' daughter, Catherine Jane. Catherine Jane, who is rebelling against her parents' rigidity and conformity, helps Rose Lee by smuggling Henry out of town when word gets around that the Klan is planning to lynch him. The leader of the local branch of the Klan is Catherine Jane's father.

In the end, the whites use the legal system to hold a bogus town-wide referendum on the issue. As a result of Jim Crow laws and fear of the Klan, the residents of Freedomtown either cannot or do not vote and therefore have no say in their future. The referendum passes, the blacks are evicted, and only Rose Lee's drawings of Freedomtown remain as a record of the tragedy.

Although the setting of *White Lilacs* is realistic, the author has created a community as closed as the farm in *Babe*. With the exception of Aunt Susannah (who grew up in Dillon) there are no outsiders in the book other than an art teacher who had moved to Dillon from Philadelphia, but she was forced to leave before the vote because of her Northern liberal views. This setting allows the author to set up the powerful against the powerless.

Rose Lee is clearly the protagonist here. She is innocent, honest, sincere, hardworking, and has an ambition to better herself. She believes in community and in the values of America. At the beginning of the book she is forgiving and has a positive view of her fellow man, black or white.

We generally get two different choices for antagonist, each of which promotes a slightly different view of the book. In most cases, people choose Mrs. Bell, Catherine Jane's mother. Of all the white people in the book, she seems to be the purest example of ignorance and selfishness. She has been rich, privileged, and sheltered her whole life. The group rarely chooses Mr. Bell, who is savvy and much more aggressive in his prejudice. This indicates that both the kids and their parents see this book as being more about the ignorance implicit in prejudice than the viciousness of it.

Curiously, the other choice of antagonist is usually Catherine Jane. Although she secretly smuggles Henry out of town, Catherine Jane does not stand up to her parents or say publicly that what she sees going on around her is wrong. Her manner is more appealing and she actually cares what happens to Rose Lee, but her solution, which is to try and make the immediate problem—Henry—disappear, does nothing to address the overall issue of pervasive discrimination.

Whether the antagonist is Catherine Jane or her mother, however, it is clear that the action that is being held back is equality for the African-American community. In either case, Freedomtown is doomed. The most important attribute of the African-American community in *White Lilacs* is its helplessness, a characteristic that is created even more by the setting than by any individual character. It will come as a great surprise to many white suburban elementary school children that as recently as the mid-twentieth century there were significant sections of the United States that legally denied basic rights to large groups of citizens based strictly on the color of their skin.

"How would you feel if you couldn't go to the same school as your friends?" we ask. "If you had to come to this book group and sit in the back, not be able to eat the snack or drink from the same water fountain?"

So, just as the setting in *Babe* announces that everything is somehow going to work out well in the end, the setting in *White Lilacs* declares that it won't. The ability of characters such as Mr. Bell and his son to get away with reprehensible behavior without fear of retribution is based in setting and establishes the overall atmosphere of the book. It is the setting that tells you that nothing bad is ever going to happen to any member of the Bell family, just as it tells you that the situation for Rose Lee and her community is hopeless.

So unlike in *Babe,* where the action explains how prejudice is overcome and where, in the end, the reader is meant to feel enlightened, *White Lilacs* hammers home that prejudice is not always overcome, and here the reader should feel angry and more aware.

CHAPTER 5

CRISIS AND CONFLICT

Identifying the Climax

What all of this analysis of character and setting is heading toward is the identification of the central conflict in the book. When we first discussed protagonist and antagonist, we said that these two characters were, in effect, pushing against each other, creating conflict. Understanding the nature of this conflict is crucial to uncovering the mystery of what the book is really about.

Sometimes it isn't as easy as it seems, even in a children's book. The story may be filled with fights and arguments, yet none of these may represent the key conflict. To help kids understand the difference, we help them to find the climax of the story.

The climax is that moment in the book to which everything is building, and after which events become inevitable. It generally does not take place at the end, as most people believe, but somewhere in the middle. To demonstrate, we talk about Shakespeare. We have found that even most second graders have heard of Shakespeare and know about plays.

"So," we ask, "why did Shakespeare write plays in five acts?"

To answer the question, we draw this:

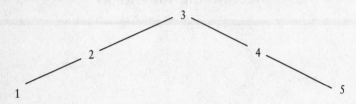

"Shakespeare uses the first act," we say, "to introduce his characters, and then, in the second act, he throws them together and lets the conflict build. In the third act, the conflict boils over, the climax is reached, and the protagonist (and often the antagonist) is changed forever. In the fourth act, we see the impact of the climax on the characters, and in the fifth act, we find out what happens to everyone.

"So, for example, in *Romeo and Juliet*," a play most kids have heard of, "Romeo and Juliet meet at a party and fall in love in the first act, and then sneak off to get married in the second act. In the third act, the climax occurs when Tybalt, one of Juliet's relatives, stabs Romeo's best friend and Romeo responds by killing Tybalt. Once Romeo commits this act, an unhappy ending becomes inevitable. The fourth act is a lot of scrambling around trying to prevent the inevitable, and in the fifth act," we conclude, "everybody dies."

In most children's books, identifying the climax is pretty easy. The children know, for example, that Ma's death, which forces Fly to say "please" to the sheep, is the climax of *Babe: The Gallant Pig*. In *Charlotte's Web*, it is Wilbur's desperate confrontation with Templeton in order to get Charlotte's egg sac back to the Zuckermans' farm, prompting Charlotte to reflect that, by helping Wilbur, she has lifted her life a little.

To illustrate this concept, and to demonstrate that no rule is inviolate, we're going to use a book where the climax occurs at the end. It's an important book by E. L. Konigsburg, one of the best children's writers around, and one that every elementary school child should read.

From the Mixed-up Files of Mrs. Basil E. Frankweiler

This is one of our favorite books. It is the story of a brother and sister, Claudia and Jamie Kincaid, who run away from their home in Greenwich, Connecticut, in order to spend a week at the Metropolitan Museum of Art in New York City. Claudia, who is twelve, plans the trip and takes nine-year-old Jamie along for company and for the money he has earned cheating at cards on the school bus. Claudia's reason for leaving is that she is not appreciated at home— as the eldest of four children she has the most chores to do—but really she is dissatisfied with herself and doesn't know why. Jamie goes along for the adventure.

They hide out at the Metropolitan Museum at the time that Mrs. Basil E. Frankweiler, a very rich, eccentric widow, has just made a gift of a statue of an angel that may or may not have been sculpted by Michelangelo. Claudia falls in love with the statue, which she names Angel, and decides to solve the mystery. The children spend all of their time and money researching the history of the statue and ultimately go so far as to confront Mrs. Basil E. Frankweiler in her Connecticut mansion.

This deceptively simple, appealing story camouflages a layered, complex, and extremely intelligent novel. You have to use all the tools in the book detective kit to get to what this book is really about. Protagonist, antagonist, and setting will help you get under the surface, but it is only with an understanding of the nature of the conflict that the ultimate meaning of the novel is revealed. That means identifying the climax.

With this book it is usually fun to ask the group what they think the story is really about *before* beginning the discussion. Last time we got the following:

- Even if you are the oldest child and your parents ignore you, they still love you and you shouldn't run away. (A mom.)
- Learning to think of yourself as an important person for who you are.
- If you pursue your dreams good things happen.
- You should be connected to the people around you. (A mom.)
- Growing up.
- It's okay to be goal-oriented as long as you take time to smell the roses. (A dad.)

▸ You can learn something from running away.
▸ Running away doesn't solve your problems.
▸ It is difficult being the oldest.
▸ It's okay to cheat at cards as long as you win. (A child.)

"What is the setting for *The Mixed-up Files*?" we asked.

That's an easy one—the Metropolitan Museum of Art in New York City.

"What year? Time is an important part of setting."

They look on the copyright page: 1967. (In this case, the setting was meant to coincide with the year it was written, so checking the copyright page was appropriate.)

"Why do you think the author chose the Metropolitan Museum of Art as the setting?"

This was much harder for the kids.

"Because they needed a place to stay," suggested Christina. Christina had showed up at this session with newly pierced ears and every time before she spoke, brushed her hair behind her ears.

"Is this the only place they could have hidden out in Manhattan?"

Everyone agreed it wasn't.

"The Metropolitan Museum of Art is a *big clue*!" we insisted. "It was not chosen at random. The author wants to talk about something. What is it?"

"Art," said Will hopelessly. Will liked airplanes and war.

"Yes, Will, it is art. So, let's discuss art. What is art?"

▸ Paintings
▸ Statues
▸ It's a creation.
▸ Self-expression

- Sends a message
- Makes us feel good
- Makes us feel sad
- Opens your imagination
- Inspiring
- Something beautiful
- A way of expressing the way you feel about the world around you

"Great," we said, and scribbled a funny face on a sketch pad. "Is this art?"

"Yes," said Robert, who had obviously spent many hours at school engaged in just this form of artistic endeavor.

"Oh, good. Somebody call the museum and we'll sell this to them. We can use a couple of million dollars."

"That's not the kind of art that goes in a museum," objected a dad. "Only the best art goes in a museum."

"Oh? So what makes a work of art good enough to be bought by the Metropolitan Museum of Art? How do we define great art?"

- You have to work hard.
- It has to be original.
- It has to be by a famous artist.
- It has to be truthful.
- It has to be universal.

"Hold that thought and let's move on to the protagonist, clearly Claudia. What are her characteristics?"

- Cautious about everything except money
- Likes to plan
- Doesn't feel important
- Gutsy
- Fussy

- Wants to learn about Angel
- Organized
- Bugs Jamie about his grammar

- Never gives up
- Hates to walk
- Thinks a lot of herself
- Straight A's

"There's one other thing about Claudia that's important," we said. "She's twelve. Think about what it must be like to be twelve." (The kids don't know yet and the parents have usually forgotten.) "You're still a kid, but you're also something else. You are closer to being in high school, for instance, to going to college, to driving a car. You are getting closer, in other words, to being a *grown-up*. But you're not quite there yet. Do you think that makes a difference? Do you think that might cause uncertainty, a kind of restlessness? When Claudia thinks of herself as not running away from home but running *to* someplace, what kind of place might that be? Does she mean a physical place, like the Met, or perhaps a state of mind, like running toward being an adult?"

Everyone agreed that this might be the case, but they also pointed out that Claudia didn't really recognize this about herself. Claudia, the kids observed, thinks her parents are ignoring her, that she has too many chores because she's the eldest, that her youngest brother gets too much attention, and that all of this is unfair.

"But she does know that she wants to be different," we said. "She just doesn't know why that is or how to *be* different. When she runs away, what she's trying to run away from most is herself. But here's the question: Is it possible

to run away from yourself? Can you change yourself simply by changing your location?"

No, everyone agreed.

"That brings us back to the art museum. If you *are*
bored with yourself and don't really know what's wrong,
wouldn't going to a place that is inspiring, that opens up
your imagination, contains beautiful things, makes you
feel good or sad, is truthful, universal, and original be helpful? Did Claudia make a good choice?"

"Yes," said Nicole. Nicole, sitting next to Christina,
kept glancing at Christina's ears with distinct envy. "You
can use your imagination at the art museum and that might
make you feel better."

"Maybe you can't change yourself on the inside simply
by changing your location but you *can* run to a place that
will help," agreed her mom.

In *The Mixed-up Files,* the selection of the antagonist is
not obvious. When we asked for a vote, we got this:

- Jamie (6)
- Mrs. Basil E. Frankweiler (3)
- Her parents (3)
- The butler did it. (1)
- The guards at the museum (0)

"Jamie. Why Jamie?"

"Because he wants to go home and Claudia doesn't,"
mumbled Evan, showering the floor in front of him with
vestiges of the snack, which we, jacks of all trades, would
be required to carpet sweep up after the session.

"Because he holds the money and won't let her buy whatever she wants," said Christina, after the obligatory hair flip.

"So Claudia as protagonist is pushing forward the action of not going home, and Jamie is trying to hold back that action? Or Claudia is pushing forward the action of spending money and Jamie is holding her back? Does that sound like what the book is about? Besides, when Claudia tells Jamie to buy tickets to Farmington, Connecticut, where Mrs. Basil E. Frankweiler lives, instead of back home to Greenwich, doesn't he buy them? In fact, doesn't the book say that for the first time he bought something without asking what it cost?"

The kids admitted this was true.

"Maybe it will help if we figure out what action Claudia *is* pushing forward. Any ideas?"

"She's trying to find out if Michelangelo made the statue," Robert's mom suggested.

"Yes," we said. "There's a part in the book when Claudia thinks, 'Angel was the way. An answer to running away, also to going home again, lay in Angel.' Why do you think this is so important to her?"

Silence.

"Well, it would seem to have something to do with Michelangelo, since Claudia is so determined to find out if he was the sculptor and the museum and the newspapers make such a big deal about him. Mrs. Basil E. Frankweiler, who, as the narrator of the story is kind of a stand-in for the author, mentions Michelangelo when she is talking to her lawyer, Saxonberg. Can anybody find what she says?"

" 'Are you altogether unconscious of the magic of the name of Michelangelo? I truly believe that his name has magic even now, the best kind of magic because it comes from true greatness. Claudia sensed it as she again stood in line. The mystery only intrigued her; the magic trapped her,' " one of the boys read.

" 'The magic' to which Mrs. Basil E. Frankweiler refers is Michelangelo's standing as one of the most important artists of the Renaissance. The Renaissance, which means 'rebirth,' " we explained, "happened about five hundred years ago. It was one of the great periods in history, when there were all sorts of thrilling new ideas in science, literature, and philosophy. And even though this Renaissance occurred in many different fields, there was one field in which the change was so amazing and fertile that it dominated all the others. And that field was art.

"The Renaissance is still known for its art and artists— Leonardo da Vinci, Raphael, Titian," we continued. "These incredibly talented people saw the world differently and this was captured in their work. And arguably the number one artist operating during this, the number one artistic period of all time was . . . Michelangelo.

"Michelangelo was a unique combination of incredible talent and single-minded commitment. It is common today to watch people who do incredible things and think that it is easy for them, that they were born with the talent and that is all it takes. Americans look at someone like Michael Jordan this way. But talent isn't enough to produce a Michael Jordan or a Michelangelo. You have to work very, very hard as well. You have to learn and keep learning and keep trying and keep working." This is a very valuable lesson for children. "The greatest people in history—Isaac Newton, Albert Einstein, Mozart, even Michael Jordan—what set them apart was not just their talent, but how hard they worked. And no one worked harder than Michelangelo.

"When he was painting the ceiling of the Sistine Chapel, Michelangelo was in despair. It was incredibly difficult, painstaking work that took four years. But he kept going despite his despair, and when he was all finished, and people came to see his work, it was so beautiful that they couldn't speak." ("I loved the history," Will came up and told us shyly after this discussion was over.)

"So," we concluded, "the statue of Angel in *The Mixed-up Files* is like a part of Michelangelo that he left behind to inspire the rest of us, to remind us of what is possible. It is this that Claudia senses. This is what drives her, and it is at the core of the book. So how does Claudia go about the task she has set for herself of finding out whether Michelangelo in fact carved Angel?"

She goes to the library, someone said. She reads books. She does research. She learns. She doesn't learn everything, the way she thinks she can at first, but she does learn. Claudia works just as hard at finding out about Angel as she would have if she were studying this subject in school. In fact, she works harder and learns more than she might have in school because she is so motivated. "I keep telling you that often the search proves more profitable than the goal," writes Mrs. Basil E. Frankweiler.

"And doesn't Jamie learn as well, even though he only

looks at the pictures in the books? Isn't it from one of those pictures that Jamie recognizes the mark on the cushion after they move Angel at the museum?"

So then we went on to talk about whether Jamie could be the antagonist if he actually helped Claudia with her research. Just because he didn't have the same need to find out if Michelangelo was the sculptor as she did, did that mean he was holding her back?

When the group realized that Jamie could not be the antagonist, we went back to why Claudia wanted to find out so badly if Michelangelo did the sculpture. After a bit of discussion, we came to the idea that Claudia thought this discovery would make her different.

"Yes, but how, exactly? What's her plan? She has a plan, doesn't she? What does she think is going to happen when she finds out?"

"Her plan is to announce her discovery to the world," said Evan's father. "She envisions reporters on her doorstep."

"She thinks she'll be famous," said Robert.

"Yes," we said. "She wants to come home as a big celebrity. She wants to impress her family with her discovery. She wants to show everyone that she is an important person. She thinks that will make her different. So who holds back Claudia's desire to become famous for her discovery? Who makes it as hard as possible for her to find out if Angel was carved by Michelangelo, and then demands secrecy?"

By this time everyone got it. Mrs. Basil E. Frankweiler was the antagonist. She's the antagonist because she holds back Claudia's mistaken craving to use her effort to gain public fame. Mrs. Frankweiler says, "I admired her spirit; but more, I wanted to help her see the value of her adventure. She still saw it as buying her something: appreciation first, information now." That is the essential conflict in the book, between achievement for public acceptance or praise, or effort for its own sake—for the personal satisfaction of knowing that you have struggled and stretched yourself and overcome something, the best achievement of all.

After all, what difference does it make what other people think? In this book, if Claudia had gotten her way, reporters would have come and made a big fuss over her. But then a day later they would be off making a big fuss over someone else. Can anyone but Claudia really understand the kind of effort it took to make the discovery?

"If Mrs. Basil E. Frankweiler is the antagonist, when does the climax occur? To which scene is everything building?"

Nicole said, "When Claudia and Jamie have to look through Mrs. Frankweiler's files to find the answer."

"Yes!" we said. "Because that was where Claudia realized that what distinguishes people from one another is effort, what they put into things. Mrs. Frankweiler made it as difficult as possible for her to find the answer, but in the end Claudia did it. She had talent, yes, but she also had commitment. That's why Claudia cries at the end. Mrs. Frankweiler specifically tells her she will not leave her the statue if she tells anyone that she knows Michelangelo sculpted it, but Claudia no longer cares. She has proved to herself that the only way to really be different is on the inside. It's the only way to find out who you really are, what you are capable of. Claudia understands that in the end.

"You know, the way Claudia felt at the beginning of the book—bored, uneasy with herself, wanting to be different—is not unique to her age," we told the kids. "You may feel that way when you are seventeen, or twenty-seven or thirty-seven or eighty. And if you feel that way, art is not the only place to turn for help. You can go to science or math or music or history or literature—anyplace where you can learn, so long as your effort is genuine. Because the act of learning helps people grow on the inside, so that you can find out who you really are and what you are capable of, just like Claudia."

CHAPTER 6

PUTTING IT TOGETHER

What Is the Book Really About?

The highlight of almost any discussion is the discovery of what the author has implanted at the core of the book. Peeling away each layer—character, setting, conflict—and finally seeing the truth is probably the most satisfying aspect of reading. It helps, of course, if there are a number of layers to work through and the author has been clever in concealment.

The benefits of discovering that a story may be more than it seems extends far beyond the scope of fiction. In a world where younger and younger children are bombarded by slogans, come-ons, and sensory assaults, it is vital to learn to evaluate the various messages that advertisers, media programmers, and even peers are promoting. Kids need to understand that the blue jeans company is not selling popularity but simply an article of clothing, and that smoking does not make you cool no matter what the pushy guy or girl in school is insisting. The only way to fully grasp these truths is to see through the hype to what is really going on—that the blue jeans are actually overpriced and ugly, or that the kids who want you to try cigarettes need followers to feel cool because they're afraid to do anything on their own.

Luckily, it is just as easy to fall into the habit of questioning as it is to fall into the habit of acceptance. For seeing through to a hidden truth, there is no better illustration than the most famous pig book of them all, George Orwell's *Animal Farm*. This is a work that is generally thought to be far too advanced for even the most talented elementary school kids, but we have had enormous success with it with fourth graders. *Animal Farm* has the advantage of a structure in which the plot is obviously a stand-in for a deeper story, but which also contains a third layer of meaning that almost no one takes the time to get to.

Animal Farm

Animal Farm, as almost every adult reader knows, is an allegory about the subversion of the Russian Revolution and the rise of Stalin. The animals of Manor Farm, following the dream of an old pig named Major (kind of an amalgam of Marx and Lenin), rise up and kick out lazy, cruel, drunken Farmer Jones and take over the farm. The leaders of the newly renamed Animal Farm are two pigs, Snowball and Napoleon (Trotsky and Stalin). In triumph, Snowball creates the seven commandments, the cornerstone of which is "All animals are equal." When Farmer Jones recruits some of his equally lazy and drunken cronies to take back his farm, the animals, led by Snowball, drive them off.

Despite Snowball's role in the great victory at the Battle of the Cowshed, Napoleon, employing a combination of propaganda and terror (a pack of vicious dogs that he raised secretly from puppyhood), soon succeeds in running Snowball off the farm and branding him an enemy of animals everywhere. Everything that goes wrong—and under Napoleon's leadership, almost everything *does* go wrong—is now blamed on Snowball who, Napoleon assures the animals, is off plotting with Farmer Jones to subvert the revolution. Little by little, Napoleon consolidates his power, eliminates his enemies, and turns the farm into a self-serving dictatorship.

Among the other animals that populate the farm are Squealer, a sneaky, cowardly pig who sucks up to Napoleon and becomes his chief of propaganda; Boxer, a loyal, hard-working horse who never loses his faith in the revolution; Boxer's friend Benjamin, a brainy donkey (and the only animal other than the pigs who can read) with no faith in the revolution or anything else; a chorus of sheep who *baaaaa* on cue to drown out dissent; and Moses, a tame raven, who is always promising the wondrous after-life of "Sugar-candy Mountain."

As Napoleon hoards all the food for himself and his cronies, the animals end up working harder and for less than they had under Farmer Jones. Even the noble, tireless Boxer eventually nears collapse under the new regime. The spirit of a revolution that promised the animals a good life drifts farther and farther away, and the seven commandments develop a habit of changing from one day to the next. At one point, Squealer is caught with a brush and a can of paint adding "But some animals are more equal than others" to "All animals are equal."

The trick with *Animal Farm* is getting through all that communist stuff early and working through the story by focusing on the characters. A brief synopsis will do.

"This story is about Russia in 1917, which is a little before most of your grandparents were born, when the country was ruled by someone called a tsar. Does anyone know what that is?"

Someone always says a kind of king.

"Is a king elected?"

No.

"Can a king's subjects tell the king that they don't like what he's doing and that they want a new king, or even no king at all?"

No.

"The tsar in Russia in 1917 was very rich but didn't do any work. What character in the story is like that?"

Farmer Jones.

"What if the tsar was mistreating the people like Farmer Jones was mistreating the animals? What could they do to make him stop?"

If the kids don't come up with the idea of revolution on their own, we eventually work them around to it. From there we simply tell them that there was a revolution in Russia in 1917. A group called the Bolsheviks rallied the poor, kicked out the tsar, and declared that Russia was free and all Russians were now equal.

After a few years of great hope and promise, the leader of the revolution, a man named Lenin, died. Two other men fought for who would be the next leader of the new, free Russia, where all the animals, uh, people, were now equal. One of the men was named Leon Trotsky and the other was named Joseph Stalin. Trotsky was a great war hero and Lenin's choice to lead the country. Trotsky was very idealistic. Stalin was ambitious and clever but little more than a thug.

Eventually, Stalin, employing a combination of propaganda and terror (a secret police that he nurtured from the early days of the revolution) won out and Trotsky was forced to leave Russia and flee to Mexico. Everything that went wrong—and under Stalin's leadership, almost everything *did* go wrong—was now blamed on Trotsky who, Stalin assured the people, was off plotting with the tsar's sympathizers to subvert the revolution. Little by little, Stalin consolidated his power, eliminated his enemies, and turned Russia into a self-serving dictatorship. The poor ended up working harder and for less than they had under the tsar.

The concept of a dictator is pretty easy to get across. Most fourth-grade kids will not have really heard of Stalin, but they will have heard of Hitler. If that fails, there is always a dictator of the moment, like Saddam Hussein. Everyone, of course, will immediately understand that Trotsky and Stalin are Snowball and Napoleon, and that all the other animals are the Russian people.

"Why does the author use different animals? Why not make them all pigs?"

This one usually stumps the kids at first, but at least some of the adults understand that different animals stand in for different kinds of Russians. This is a vital point, because it will come back later.

"So, for example, what do you think Moses the Raven represents and what is this 'Sugarcandy Mountain' that he says they'll go to after they die?"

The kids usually don't get Moses right off, but we can pretty easily get them to see that Sugarcandy Mountain is a kind of heaven, and from there we can work back to Moses representing the Church.

"What about Boxer?"

That one is easy. Boxer represents the workers.

"Benjamin?"

This is generally the most difficult for both the kids and the adults. That Orwell made Benjamin a donkey tends to throw them. The way to get to Benjamin is to remind them that he is the only nonpig who can read.

"The smart people?" a kid will generally guess, followed by a parent who'll say, "The intellectuals?"

We have found that it is important here to take a few minutes and describe what Orwell meant by intellectuals, that in Russia there were people who were very educated and who lived pretty well under the tsar even though they didn't necessarily do a lot of work. They usually thought politics was beneath them (according to Orwell) and didn't especially care what was happening to the people, either before or after the revolution.

"So, a story like this is called an allegory. Does anyone know what that is?"

Surprisingly, there always seems to be a kid who does. When there isn't, we refer to books such as *Babe* or *Charlotte's Web* (keeping the pig metaphor intact) where, even though the animal characters don't represent actual historical figures, they are given human personalities.

Once we establish that *Animal Farm* is a story where animals (and the occasional human) stand in for people in history, we always discuss why an author would choose to populate a story with animals instead of humans. When we first did this, we were surprised at how insightful the kids were.

"It makes the story funny," said Jordan.

"But is this a funny story?" we asked.

Megan waved her hand furiously. "No," she replied, "but there's some funny stuff in it." Megan was one of the more unique kids we've had. From the moment she walked into the room, she never stopped moving. During the discussions, the only way she could stay in her seat was to chew on her coat. But she read every book with almost fanatical care and participated with extraordinary enthusiasm.

"Like what?"

"Squealer is funny," said Taylor. Taylor was nine and a bank president in the making. She had confided after a previous session that she intended to get all A's in every grade, otherwise she might not get into Harvard or Yale, which might keep her from getting a high-paying job.

It was soon established that the sheep were pretty funny

as well, as were the crows. Benjamin the donkey could be funny sometimes, and even Napoleon was funny after he got so fat (off the labor of the other animals) that he could hardly walk.

"So," we asked, "is it good in a serious story to have some funny stuff?"

"It can be."

"But it can't be too funny," said Megan, beating Taylor to the punch.

"Why not?"

"Because then it won't be serious anymore."

With the foundation established, we move on to the characters. Although there are generally only two nominees for protagonist, Napoleon and Snowball, choosing between them turns out to be tricky. As many times as we have told the kids that the protagonist does not have to be the hero, those who choose Snowball do so largely on the basis of his virtuous nature. He is brave, caring, and smart. He believes in the original idea that everyone is equal and should share in all the fruits of their labor. Napoleon, on the other hand, is mean, sneaky, clever, self-centered, cruel, lazy, heartless, and greedy. Yet he does somehow seem to represent the heart of the book more than does Snowball.

If the group votes for Snowball as the protagonist—and this happens a little less than half the time—we run an experiment.

"Then what action is Snowball pushing forward that Napoleon is holding back?" we ask.

"He's pushing forward the revolution."

"Freedom."

"Equality."

"So, then," we say, "this must be a book about the triumph of freedom and equality over tyranny. Does that seem right?"

Everyone will agree that that does not seem right.

"So how can Snowball be the protagonist?"

When Snowball's candidacy is grudgingly withdrawn, there doesn't seem to be any choice left except Napoleon.

When we move to antagonist, Snowball, having been rejected as protagonist, will quickly gain the support of most of the room. There are generally some other choices, too. Major, the pig who started it all, gets a couple of votes for having the dream even though he appears only in one scene. Boxer often gets a few votes because of his unselfish work ethic, as does Benjamin simply because he refuses to get involved in anything. When it comes right down to it, though, this definitely seems like a Napoleon versus Snowball book.

"How can this be?" we asked. "An evil protagonist and a heroic antagonist? What can this book *possibly* be about?"

Silence. Even Megan was stumped.

"Well, what is going on here? What action is Napoleon pushing forward?"

"He's trying to take over," said Jordan.

"He's trying to get rid of all of his enemies," said Jordan's mom.

"He's trying to get power," said Taylor, with perhaps the slightest touch of envy.

Usually, at this point, somebody gets it. "So a book

doesn't always have to be about something good," said another one of the moms.

"That's right. Is this book about something good? Does good triumph in the end here?"

No one thought so.

"So what is this book about? That crime pays?"

Nobody wanted to say so, but it did seem that it might be true.

"Maybe this is a book about how a wonderful dream was destroyed by ambition and greed?"

Maybe.

"And it happened right under the noses of those who needed most to keep that dream alive. How could they have let that happen?"

"They were tricked," cried Andrew.

"They couldn't read," said Megan.

"They were scared of the dogs," said Taylor's dad.

"They didn't understand what was happening until it was too late," said one of the other dads.

"So it was inevitable, then," we concluded. "It had to happen?"

The group didn't want to accept this but they didn't know what else to say.

"Then why did the author write the book?"

"To warn people?" said Megan.

"Yes. Maybe. But what's the point of a warning if the author's message is that there is nothing you can do about it? That must also mean that Old Major's dream was hooey all along, huh?"

If we've done our job, by this point the kids (and most

of the adults) will be completely confused. The action of the book, the hidden message, seems clear yet makes no sense. Orwell seems to be saying that it was inevitable that Napoleon would take over and corrupt Major's dream to suit his own purposes. So why indeed write a book warning people of evil if it is going to happen anyway? Is Orwell's view of the world completely cynical? *This* is a classic?

This is where we go one layer deeper.

"There was nothing wrong with old Major's dream," we said, "but having a dream is not the same thing as putting it into practice. Putting a dream into practice takes work."

"But the animals did work," said a mom. "They worked so hard that some of them died." (Invariably, the most affecting scene in the book is when the great Boxer, too weak to resist, is shipped off to the glue factory by Napoleon, who later claims, through the detestable Squealer, that it was actually the hospital.)

"Maybe Orwell was talking about a different kind of work. You said before that the animals were tricked. Were there any animals who weren't tricked, who *knew* what was going on?"

Benjamin knew. He knew all the time. He knew that the commandments were being changed. He even knew Boxer's real destination because he read the sign on the truck.

"So why didn't he do anything about it?"

"He tried to stop them from sending Boxer away," Taylor said.

"By then it was too late. What about before?"

"He didn't care. He was always saying, 'Donkeys live a long time,' " said Megan.

"What does that mean?"

That nothing was going to happen to him—or so he thought.

"If Benjamin understood what Napoleon was up to, what *should* he have done about it?"

The first reaction is always the same. "He should tell the other animals so they can stop Napoleon," said Jenny, who only spoke about once a session.

"But if he does, Napoleon might kill him," said Taylor's father.

"But Napoleon will eventually kill him anyway," noted Jordan's mother.

"Not if he gets all the animals to fight," rejoined her son.

All of a sudden, everyone agreed that Benjamin, the intellectual, should have asserted himself and tried to be a leader instead of just sitting back and doing nothing to stop what was going on. Benjamin was a respected figure, everyone listened to him. He might have succeeded against Napoleon.

"But what about the dogs?" we asked. "Wasn't Benjamin afraid of the dogs?"

There was some vague recognition in the room, but no one could put his or her finger on it, so we told them to open to chapter seven.

"*The dogs are afraid of Boxer,*" Taylor called out, referring to the scene where Boxer steps on one of the dogs and the rest run away whimpering in terror. "Boxer could have protected Benjamin."

"Only Benjamin?"

"Boxer could have protected everybody!"

"So why didn't he, even though he was strong enough?"

The kids were a little sad after someone said, "No one told him to."

So, between Benjamin and Boxer, Napoleon could have been stopped. The author did leave open the possibility that the dictatorship didn't have to happen, after all. Revolutions don't all have to end the same way. Didn't the American Revolution result in democracy?

We never stop there, however.

"Tell us, kids," we say to every group, "are there any cliques in your class?"

There always are.

"What about the leaders of the cliques? Do they exclude people, just because they feel like it?"

They always do.

"Do they pick on the kids who are weaker or a little different?"

They always do that, too.

"What about kids who aren't in the clique? Are any of them strong enough, or smart enough, or respected enough to stand up for the kids who are being picked on?"

There are always some of those kids.

"Do they stand up to the clique?"

They usually don't.

"Then doesn't that make them just as responsible for what's going on as Benjamin was?"

And so, through an allegory about an event in history about which they know little or nothing, kids can confront the age-old question: Who is more responsible, the person who perpetrates malice or the one who could have stopped it but chose instead to stand by and allow it to happen?

The fact that a book that is renowned for its political satire is actually about personal responsibility is a surprise to both kids and their parents. Most great books, regardless of how sophisticated the language or complex the plot, have, at their core, a simple theme, usually a very basic moral dilemma. These are the kinds of issues that we encounter throughout our lives. What makes great books great is that these moral questions are posed in a fair and thought-provoking way, whereas in lesser books, the characters or the story is structured so as to make resolution easy and obvious.

CHAPTER 7

WHO'S RIGHT?

Point of View

Kids are usually taught to accept as true anything they read or are told by an "authority" (any adult), so the concept of point of view will be a new one to the elementary school reader. Children need to understand that even a first-person account may be biased or inaccurate. Knowledge comes from sifting through various and often conflicting sources.

Points of view are as varied as the human experience itself. Where people were born, where they grew up, where they went to school, what their parents did for a living, who their friends and neighbors were, or even chance all contributes to who they are, what they think, and how they see the world. All of that, in turn, plays into how they communicate that vision to others. Since authors, television newspeople, politicians, athletic coaches, teachers, parents, and even grandparents are all just people, they each come equipped with their own particular bias—their point of view.

To explore this concept, we suggest *Bull Run* by Paul Fleischman, an outstanding piece of historical fiction that we do in third grade.

Bull Run

Bull Run is a fictionalized account of the opening months of the Civil War, beginning with the firing on Fort Sumter in April 1861 and ending with the battle of Bull Run—Manassas to Southerners—in July of the same year. Most of the civilians in the area (Manassas is in Virginia, just outside of Washington, D.C.) did not take the coming conflict all that seriously, and adopted an almost festive air, packing picnics and taking carriages to the site of what was supposed to be an easy Northern victory. Instead, what they got was a ferocious battle. While it appeared at first that the North would easily triumph, the South ultimately routed the Union forces. That the Confederacy prevailed was due in no small part to an obscure history-professor-turned-general named Thomas Jonathan Jackson, who either bravely or stupidly (depending on your point of view) refused to retreat and "stood there like a damned stone wall." The spectators who had brought fried chicken and champagne fled in a panic, while the field lay littered with dead and horribly wounded soldiers.

What is unusual about Fleischman's account is that he tells the story not as a linear narrative but rather through the eyes of sixteen different participants, eight from the North and eight from the South. The Southerners include a jaded colonel, a dirt-poor illiterate nineteen-year-old who enlists in the cavalry because he loves horses, a Virginia housewife, a doctor, and a young woman slave. Some of the representatives of the North are General Irvin McDowell, commander of the Army of the Potomac, and the only genuine historical figure in the novel; a Minnesota girl who loses a brother in the battle; a free black man who tries to join the Union army; a sketch artist for the *New York Illustrated News;* a freelance photographer; and a carriage driver whose job it is to ferry merrymakers to and from Washington. All these different people tell their stories and the reader has to decide what is going on by piecing together a coherent whole.

Before we begin to discuss the book itself, we spend a little time giving some background on the Civil War. Most children have at least heard of the war and may even equate it with slavery or Abraham Lincoln, although we have had many children who confused the Civil War with the American Revolution.

In one of our groups, when we asked our third graders and their parents what they knew about the Civil War, we got back this:

- Lincoln was president.
- The Southern states seceded and said they were going to be their own countries.
- It lasted four years, from 1861 to 1865.

- Lincoln wrote the Gettysburg Address.
- Before the war each state got to choose if they had slaves or not.
- The South elected Jefferson Davis as president.
- A lot of people got killed.
- The South thought they would win even though they didn't have raw materials.
- The South wanted slaves and the North didn't.
- The South was prejudiced.
- The South wanted to be independent.
- The North wanted the federal government to be more powerful.
- The North didn't think it was fair that the South had slave labor because they couldn't make as much money.

As with *Animal Farm*, we don't dwell too much on the politics. It is more important that the children understand that historical fiction, like *Bull Run*, is not the same as history. When we ask the difference, there's always someone who is going to say "historical fiction is made up," but we don't stop there.

"Any other differences?"

Historical Fiction

- A fiction book with facts in it
- Almost everybody is made up.
- The setting and details are mostly real.

History

- Was a long, long time ago
- It's about famous people.
- It's nonfiction.

"But how do we know what really happened in history? Anyone ever hear of primary and secondary sources? A primary source is a document or a picture that was written or taken at the time of the event by someone who was either a participant or present at the event. A secondary source is somebody writing about the event after the fact, based on other peoples' observations or recollections. Let's list some primary and secondary sources."

Primary Sources

- Letters
- Diaries
- Photographs
- Drawings
- Telegraph messages
- Newspapers
- Grandparents, if they were alive at the time (though not for this book, obviously)
- Bullets, guns, sabers, household items (These are technically artifacts, but we don't feel the need to make that distinction for the kids.)

Secondary Sources

▸ A nonfiction textbook
▸ The Internet (There are some primary sources reprinted on the Internet, but generally the information is compiled from secondary sources, which will be a big surprise to third graders who equate the Internet with the Oracle.)
▸ An adult history book

"So, in *Bull Run*, even though the characters are made up, the author wanted to be as realistic as possible. He used both primary and secondary sources in his research. In that way, *Bull Run* is very similar to nonfiction."

Once we have established that the setting and the details of the battle are historically accurate, it is time to move on to the characters. Fleischman himself, in a note at the end, suggests that it might be worthwhile to stage this as a play or reader's theater, and we take him at his word. In our previous session, we had put all the characters' names in a big hat and assigned parts at random so that we could interview the characters to find out their role in the battle and how each of them feel about the war. With sixteen characters to go through, there obviously isn't room to detail each discussion here, so we'll outline five characters to give a sense of what we do. Our five are Gideon Adams, the free black man who wants to fight on the side of the Union; Carlotta King, the slave from Mississippi; James Dacy, the sketch artist for the illustrated newspaper;

Nathaniel Epp, the freelance photographer; and Judah Jenkins, a Confederate courier.

"Gideon Adams, would you come down, please?"

Whoever is playing Gideon comes and takes a seat next to us at the front of the room.

"Gideon, it's so nice to see you today. Thank you for agreeing to this interview. Tell me, Gideon, where are you from?"

Gideon is from Ohio.

"How do the white people treat you in Ohio?"

They treat Gideon and other free black men badly. When Gideon and his friends tried to recruit black soldiers for the Union army, drunken, club-wielding white men told them to go back to their miserable homes. (If Gideon cannot tell us this right away, we have him look at pages seven and eight of the book.)

"Really! Ohio is in the South, then? That's how they treat black people in the South, isn't it?"

Gideon should be pretty sure that Ohio is in the North. If he is not, we tell him to refer to the map at the beginning of the book.

"Gideon, do you mean to say that there were many white people in the North who treated black people badly? Who didn't respect them, who didn't think they could fight, who didn't really regard them as equals?"

Gideon should suspect that this is true.

"What happened next? On page fifteen it says that you and three of your friends tried to join the infantry the next day. What happened?"

Lawrence and Nancy Goldstone

Neither Gideon nor his friends were allowed to join as soldiers because they were black.

"What did your friends do?"

Some took menial jobs like cooking or ditch-digging. Others went home.

"You didn't do that, though, did you? What did you do?"

Gideon pretended to be white by cutting off all of his hair, putting on a cap, and assuming a new name.

"Did it work?"

It did.

"What did the recruiter say?"

He said that Gideon would be paid thirteen dollars a month to sign up for ninety days, which was more than enough time to whip the Rebels.

"How do you feel about your decision to masquerade as a white man?"

Gideon does not feel good about it. He's worried about it. He's afraid the other soldiers will find out. He's scared.

"But you went through with it anyway, right?"

Yes.

"So what is it like in the regiment? What are the other soldiers like?"

Gideon should read from page thirty-nine:

Oftentimes I felt I must have joined the Southern army by mistake. The soldiers mercilessly abused a stuttering black cook in our company. . . . Some declared they'd rather shoot Negroes than the Rebels.

"So, all these other white soldiers, they aren't fighting for the same reason you are. Why are you fighting again?"

To free the slaves.

"Do these other soldiers care about slaves or black people?"

No.

"Okay, Gideon. Hold that thought, and thank you for your time. Will Carlotta King come down, please?"

Carlotta King takes a seat next to us.

"Carlotta, could you tell us something about yourself, please?"

Carlotta tells us that she is a slave from Mississippi.

"Then what are you doing here at Bull Run?"

Carlotta explains that her master joined the Confederate army. She washes and cooks for him. Many Confederate soldiers came to Bull Run with their slaves.

"How do you feel about the war, Carlotta?"

Carlotta is in favor of the war. She thinks the Yankees are there to free the slaves. She knows the Union troops are just a few miles away. She wants to run away from her master and cross over to the North and freedom.

"What's stopping you? Why don't you do it?"

Because another slave told her that she had tried to escape and that the Yankees had caught her and returned her to her master.

"What? Can that possibly be true? That Northern troops returned slaves?"

Carlotta is confused.

"Didn't the author research this book like it was history? Doesn't that mean that there must have been instances when this was true?"

Carlotta thinks it must be so.

"Anybody here ever hear of the Fugitive Slave Act? The Fugitive Slave Act was a law passed before the Civil War. It said that if a slave ran away from his or her master in the South, whoever discovered that slave in the North had to hand him back. If you didn't, you went to jail. The Fugitive Slave Act was not popular in the North and in fact was one of several important events that resulted in the war, but many people obeyed it anyway. The Yankees did hand back runaway slaves. How do you feel about that, Carlotta?"

It made her sick.

"So you didn't run away?"

She decided to wait and see how the battle turned out. At first, she thought the North won and she wanted to yell for joy. But then she found out the South won.

"So what did you do then?"

Carlotta ran away but decided to steer clear of Union soldiers so they didn't send her back.

"Thank you, Carlotta. You've been very helpful. Will James Dacy please come forward? Thank you for joining us, James. We understand you are an educated man. Please tell us about yourself."

James Dacy is an artist covering the war for the *New York Illustrated News*.

"New York. Would that be the North or the South?"

The North.

"What's your job exactly?"

James is traveling with the Sixth Massachusetts Regiment, the first to leave for Washington. "I was to send back drawings that would let readers stand where I stood and view the war as if there, lacking naught but the singing of bullets past their ears," as it says on page eleven.

"James! That makes you a primary source, doesn't it? You're going to be one of those people all of us historians read later to try and figure out what happened."

Yes, now that we mention it, that seems to be what James is.

"So how's the war going?"

It started out pretty well, says James. There was a lot of excitement and a big send-off when the regiment first left Boston by train. The same was true in New York, where the regiment marched down Broadway to cheering crowds.

"Then you went to Baltimore, right? Where is Baltimore, anyway?"

If James doesn't know, consult the map.

"Maryland. What happened in Maryland?"

The troops were attacked by a mob wearing Confederate ribbons. At first they threw rotting vegetables and rocks, but then somebody shot at them and they had to shoot back.

"My goodness! Maryland must be in the South, right? Fought on the Confederate side?"

James isn't sure. Check the map again. Maryland is a border state.

"A border state. What's that?"

James doesn't know.

"Border states were those that border the seceding

states, but did not secede themselves. However, because they were so close to the South, sentiment in those states was very mixed. Many people supported the Southern cause, as James discovered. Right, James?"

Right.

"So you drew a picture for the newspaper of that mob in Baltimore, right, James? You let the readers stand where you stood, and all that?"

No, James did not draw a picture.

"Why not?"

He was so angry his hands were shaking.

"That's a pity, missing an important historical event like that. But that's not the only drawing you missed, is it? Didn't you neglect to put something else in?"

If James draws a blank here, have him look at page thirty-two. James had just finished drawing a regiment going through its drills and was exceedingly enthusiastic about Union prospects for victory. But then he went for a walk and saw a Union officer reading a book and "practicing shouting orders *to the trees*. The scene filled me with foreboding. I declined to present it to the readers of the *New York Illustrated News*."

"James! Are you sure you're doing your job? Are you giving an objective picture of the war to your readers?"

James admits that he isn't.

"So anyone who looks at your sketches and thinks they're seeing things as they are would be wrong?"

Yes.

"And that goes not just for people now, when the war is

being fought, but later when people study the war, doesn't it? You're misleading everyone in the future, too, aren't you?"

James admits that he is.

"Even people in that third-grade parent-child book group at the library!"

James is downcast.

"James, we really hate to say this, but we think you are biased. Do you know what biased means?"

Frequently, James does not.

"It means that you have a particular point of view—in this case, a pro-Union perspective. You do not even *try* for objectivity! You are letting your feelings get in the way of your job!"

Well, yes, James thinks that, too.

"Well, thank goodness that at least journalism has changed since the days of the Civil War. There aren't any journalists today who have a bias, are there? When we hear the news, we're getting a completely objective version, right? Newspaper reports and television commentators and especially all those people who talk about politics on cable television networks, they're telling the unvarnished truth, right? There's no bias today, is there?"

By this time, the parents are laughing and most kids get it.

"Well, thank you for your honesty, James. You did a good job. Will Nathaniel Epp please come here? Nathaniel, thank you for taking the time to talk to us. Would you please tell us your current occupation?"

Nathaniel is a photographer.

"A photographer. Another primary source! So you work for a newspaper, like Mr. Dacy?"

No, Nathaniel does not work for a newspaper. He works for himself.

"What exactly do you take photographs of, Nathaniel?"

Nathaniel takes portraits of people and sells them as souvenirs.

"Where are you as the book opens, Nathaniel?"

Nathaniel is in Washington, D.C.

"What brought you to Washington?"

There were thousands of soldiers in Washington and Nathaniel knows that he can take a lot of photographs and sell a lot of portraits.

"Is there a particular photo you want to tell us about?"

If Nathaniel does not know, have him look at page twenty. He should then be able to tell you that he was taking a photograph of a soldier when somebody fired a gun by accident and shot him, so that he fell to the ground just as Nathaniel was taking the picture. In the book, Nathaniel goes on to report:

I thought the portrait ruined by his moving, but developed it out of respect. It showed a blurry human shape seeming to step out of the standing man's skin . . . that evening, I did a brisk business, at ten cents a head, in exhibiting what I billed to be the first photograph of the human soul, plainly leaving a dying body. I have never gone hungry since.

"Nathaniel! You're not making a profit on the war, are you?"

It would appear that Nathaniel was.

"Isn't that taking advantage of the soldiers?"

Well, yes, sort of.

"What exactly is your interest in the war, Nathaniel? Whose side are you on?"

Nathaniel isn't sure. He doesn't seem to be on any side.

"Do you mean to say that the author of this book is pointing out that there were some people who liked the war because they *made money* on it? With so much at stake, they were only interested in it for personal gain? Were you like that, Nathaniel?"

Nathaniel isn't too happy with himself either.

"Thank you for your help, Nathaniel. You may sit down. Will Judah Jenkins please come forward? Thank you for joining us, Judah. Tell us, where are you from?"

Judah is from Alexandria.

"Where's that?"

Alexandria is in Virginia, near Washington, D.C.

"So you're what—a Northerner or Southerner?"

Judah is a Southerner.

"In the Confederate army?"

He is now. He wasn't in the beginning. He wasn't too sure about secession.

"What convinced you to join the Confederacy? Are you fighting to keep your slaves?"

If Judah does not know the answer to this, have him look at pages thirty-three and thirty-four. There he will discover that he decided to join the Confederacy after witnessing a Northern colonel taking a Confederate flag off a hotel roof. The colonel was shot by the hotel owner for stealing the property, and the hotel owner was in turn gunned down and bayoneted by one of the colonel's men. That very evening Judah joined the Confederates.

"Why is this incident so important to you, Judah?"

Judah is not sure. But he knows he didn't like watching the hotel owner get killed so brutally.

"Did you call the Northerners invaders?"

Judah did.

"So you feel invaded, like you have no choice but to fight? That the North is being brutal and coming in and stealing your stuff and you have to fight them? It doesn't matter why, you just can't let them walk in and do that?"

Yes, Judah agrees, that all sounds right.

"Thank you, Judah. You may sit down."

When we are done with the characters, we ask the group what this Civil War book is all about. What is the message here? How can we find a message with no protagonist or antagonist? Doesn't that mean that there's no conflict?

Hands go up all over the room.

"There *is* conflict."

"Everybody has a different point of view."

"The Northerners hate the Southerners. The Southerners hate the Northerners."

"There's no interest in or sympathy for black people on either side."

"So what's going on?" we ask again. "Why is everybody fighting?"

If we've done our job, the kids and the parents will see that there is no one truth. How you regarded the Civil War and the battle of Bull Run had a lot to do with who you were and the point of view that you brought to the event.

"But this is fiction, right? That's why there are so many interpretations. In real life, in real history, we know what happened, right? Everybody agrees."

By this time the group is not so sure, so we read them John Godfrey Saxe's famous poem "The Blind Men and the Elephant," which he based on an Indian legend.

THE BLIND MEN AND THE ELEPHANT

It was six men of Indostan,
To learning much inclined,
Who went to see the elephant
(Though all of them were blind),
That each by observation
Might satisfy his mind.

The first approached the elephant,
And, happening to fall
Against his broad and sturdy side,
At once began to bawl:
"God bless me! but the elephant
Is very like a wall!"

The second, feeling of the tusk,
Cried: "Ho! what have we here
So very round and smooth and sharp?

To me 'tis mighty clear
This wonder of an elephant
Is very like a spear!"

The third approached the animal,
And, happening to take
The squirming trunk within his hands,
Thus boldly up and spake:
"I see," quoth he, "the elephant
Is very like a snake!"

The fourth reached out his eager hand,
And felt about the knee:
"What most this wondrous beast is like
Is mighty plain," quoth he;
" 'Tis clear enough the elephant
Is very like a tree!"

The fifth, who chanced to touch the ear,
Said: "E'en the blindest man
Can tell what this resembles most;
Deny the fact who can,
This marvel of an elephant
Is very like a fan!"

The sixth no sooner had begun
About the beast to grope,
Than, seizing on the swinging tail
That fell within his scope,

"I see," quoth he, "the elephant
Is very like a rope!"

And so these men of Indostan
Disputed loud and long,
Each in his own opinion
Exceeding stiff and strong,
*Though each was partly in the right
And all were in the wrong!*

Every historical event (and current event as well) is just like the poem and just like *Bull Run*. Truth is how you see things, or how it is presented to you. Even a firsthand account of an event—one of those primary sources—may be biased. The more evidence one has, the more points of view one is exposed to, the deeper the understanding and the richer the perspective will be.

Understanding point of view sometimes reveals some curiously interesting, and unintended, aspects of a story.

Lost Horizon

Lost Horizon is one of the most popular books ever written. When it first came out in 1933, so many copies were sold that its publisher created a low-priced mass-market paperback, the first of its kind, to meet demand. Five years later it was made into an equally popular film by Frank

Capra who is known for such heartwarming classics as *It's a Wonderful Life* and *Mr. Deeds Goes to Town.*

The secret of *Lost Horizon*'s popularity lay in the period in which it was written. The United States and much of the world was mired in depression. Millions of Americans were out of work or barely limping by. People who had worked all their lives were suddenly forced to stand in bread lines in order to feed their families and to live in shantytowns to have a roof over their heads. Thousands of small farmers were forced off their land.

In Europe, Adolf Hitler had just been appointed chancellor of Germany. Stalin (the kids know who he is now) was in power in Russia. Spain was on the verge of civil war. And as bad as conditions were, it seemed that they were only going to get worse. Even Franklin Delano Roosevelt's buoyant optimism could not relieve the national sense of despair. Many Americans sought escape in books and movies, especially madcap comedies, musicals, stories of the nobility of the common man, and most of all, tales of hope.

Lost Horizon is the story of Robert Conway, a disillusioned English World War I veteran. As the story opens, Conway is now a member of the British Foreign Service stationed in Baskul, a remote outpost in India in the throes of civil war. The rebel troops are about to overrun the city and there is panic everywhere as both the native and European populations desperately attempt to flee. After helping hundreds make their escape, Conway, in the very last moments before the town is taken, secures a plane to evacuate Mallinson, a young British officer; Barnard, a mysterious American; Mrs. Brinklow, an English missionary; and himself.

When the plane takes off, however, the passengers notice that the pilot, rather than the British flying officer they were expecting, is an Asian. Instead of flying west toward Europe, he takes them east, toward the Himalayas. After a mysterious stop to refuel at a Mongolian village, the plane eventually crashes high in the mountains. The pilot is killed and the four passengers are marooned in a cold, snowy wasteland. Suddenly, out of nowhere appears an exotic caravan led by a seemingly ageless man named Chang, who leads the group through a treacherous pass to a warm, sunlit valley. Dominated at one end by a huge peak called Karakal, the Valley of the Blue Moon, as it is called, is the home of a monastery known as Shangri-La.

Everyone in Shangri-La seems remarkably happy, industrious, and peaceful, but Chang refuses to answer questions about the monastery's origin or the unusual climate. Of the four, Conway is most taken with his surroundings and feels a contentment that he has never felt before. Barnard, who is actually a stock swindler on the run, is in no hurry to leave, and Mrs. Brinklow is resigned to wait for as long as it takes. Only Mallinson is agitated and upset—he constantly and obnoxiously badgers Conway to "do something" and wants to leave immediately. He believes they have been kidnapped and are being held prisoner. Conway replies that if they are being held prisoner, it is a very comfortable captivity.

Mallinson finally prevails upon Conway to discharge his responsibilities as a British officer and find a way for the four to return to civilization. Conway is told by Chang that only the High Lama can make that decision. Chang also tells Conway the history of Shangri-La, which was founded over two centuries before by a remarkable Belgian priest named Father Perreault.

Conway is eventually summoned before the High Lama, an unprecedented honor according to Chang, and discovers the secret of Shangri-La. The High Lama is actually Father Perreault himself, now over two hundred years old. Father Perreault reveals not only that the Valley of the Blue Moon has strange properties that retard aging (only for Europeans, not the Tibetan natives) but that he has founded Shangri-La in order to put into effect his vision of a better world. He expects the "civilized" world to destroy itself and he has spent his time accumulating the great treasures of mankind—art, books, music, and such—so that when that time comes, Shangri-La will be the new beginning. "And the meek will surely inherit the earth." In order to maintain the secret of Shangri-La, no one in the community is allowed to leave, a needless prohibition according to Father Perreault, since no one has ever wanted to.

In subsequent meetings Father Perreault tells Conway that he is about to die and he has chosen Conway as his successor. Conway, who for the first time has found peace, accepts. But Mallinson convinces him that he has been hoodwinked by a lunatic and that his real duty is to escape. To prove his point, Mallinson offers a beautiful Chinese woman named Lo Tsen, who looks twenty although Chang claims she is very old. Conway agrees to leave with Mallinson and Lo Tsen. When next seen, Conway is in a hospital somewhere in China, having been brought there with an extremely old Chinese woman. Mallinson is dead.

Conway soon escapes from the hospital and then performs superhuman acts to once again find the Valley of the Blue Moon.

When we asked our fifth-grade group to list potential protagonists and antagonists in the story, most of the group immediately chose Conway, a few went for Father Perreault, and there was one vote for Chang. The group quickly decided, however, that Conway, Chang, and Father Perreault all represented much the same thing—hope and the promise of a better world in Shangri-La. Mallinson, they added, was clearly the antagonist, representing everything that is greedy, selfish, and self-destructive about modern civilization.

"That's not right," said Rebecca. "Shangri-La isn't a good place. It's a dictatorship."

"That's right," said her father. This was the first time in about three years that they had genuinely agreed on anything. "It doesn't matter how pleasant it is. It's just like taking drugs. It seems pleasant, but once you start, you're hooked. If anyone changed their mind and decided they didn't like Shangri-La, they were stuck. The High Lama makes all the decisions. They've stolen the books and art from a world that needed them."

"So who's the protagonist?"

"Mallinson," said Rebecca.

"Mallinson?" we exclaimed. "But he's obnoxious. To say nothing of the fact that he calls the Chinese 'Chinks.' What action is he pushing forward?"

"He wants freedom," she insisted.

"Right," said her father. "It doesn't matter that he isn't

charming. He wants his freedom and he's willing to fight for it."

"And Conway?"

"He must be the antagonist," said Paul, a boy who had originally thought Conway the protagonist. "He wants everybody to be happy with no freedom at all."

"So then, if Conway or Chang or Father Perreault is the protagonist, the book is about hope and if Mallinson is the protagonist, the book is about drug addiction?"

Mallinson was getting more votes by the minute.

"But wait a second. Do you think that is what the author had in mind?" we asked. "Do you think he intentionally wrote a book that seemed to be about this cool place of hope, but was secretly telling everyone to resist dictatorship, no matter how pleasant it appeared on the surface?"

It was either that, said Rebecca's father, or he didn't realize what he was writing.

If James Hilton didn't realize what he was writing, neither did the millions and millions of readers who gobbled up edition after edition looking at Shangri-La as a wonderful fantasy in a grim and despairing world. In fact, the term *Shangri-La* itself entered the language as a synonym for utopia.

"So why," we asked the group, "do some of us see the book so differently today?"

From here, it was easy to get into a discussion about why people would grasp at a fantasy and under what circumstances. In 1933, people were hungry and it looked like war was coming. What they wanted most was peace, to feel safe in their homes, and to have their basic human needs met. To achieve these things, many people were willing to give up the right to vote and the right to travel. Or maybe they just didn't think much about it while they were feeling scared and weak.

The difference in the interpretation could be that modern society has lived through Hitler and Stalin. Perhaps we have learned to distrust people who promise utopia if only they are allowed to run things unconditionally.

Or maybe we haven't come as far as we think. Who would be willing to rewrite the Constitution to protect us from, say, another September 11? Isn't there a dialogue going on in America today about how much of our freedom we are willing to give up in order to protect ourselves from terror? How do we feel about giving up *our* freedom in exchange for security? What if you are the person who is not allowed to get on the plane because you look different and the other people are frightened of you? What if people stop speaking to you and start staring at you because they suspect your allegiance? Is it worth it to give up your freedom then?

Wherever the discussion goes, *Lost Horizon* is a book rich with the possibilities of helping both kids and parents understand not only a past era, but the one we live in now.

CHAPTER 8

OBVIOUS CHARACTERS, CONTRIVED ENDINGS, AND CONVENIENT PLOT DEVICES

Grading the Author

Kids spend a good deal of their time being judged, but are rarely given the feeling that adults care what they think. When we move into the literary courtroom for the final step, critical evaluation, we encourage children to bring their own judgments to questions such as the author's skill or fairness.

To illustrate, let's return to *White Lilacs,* the historical novel about the destruction of the black community in Texas. By the end of the discussion, there is almost always a consensus that Carolyn Meyer's point of view was clear: a greedy, selfish, unfeeling white population in the 1920s South was willing to uproot African-American families, destroy their communities, and violate the spirit, if not the letter, of the law to obtain a petty convenience. This, the group further agrees, is a condemnation of the entire town and, by implication, white people in general in the 1920s South.

When we ask the group if this portrait agrees with what they know of American history, every fourth grader we have had says that it does. *White Lilacs,* therefore, is a powerful reinforcement of what the kids have been taught both at school and in their homes about a shameful period in our nation's history.

Then we tell everyone to turn to the back of the book.

In a postscript, Ms. Meyer discussed how she had come to write *White Lilacs.* She mentions that, in 1991, having just moved to Denton, Texas, she attended the dedication of a plaque in the city park. We then ask one of the kids to read aloud what the plaque said.

On this site from the late 19th century until 1922 stood the thriving community of Quakertown. This African-American community was founded in the years following Reconstruction and was named, according to one account, to honor the Abolitionist Pennsylvania Quakers. In its heyday, Quakertown contained fifty-eight families, stores, restaurants, a doctor's office, a mortuary, and three churches. In April of 1921, a bond election was held to raise $75,000, to create a city park on the 27 acre Quakertown site. In spite of opposition from the residents, this proposal passed 367 to 240. By 1923, the residents of Quakertown were required to move. Many of these families moved to the Solomon Hill and Hiram additions to East Denton. The former Quakertown residents and their descendants continue to contribute to the community life of Denton.

When the child is done, we ask if anyone had noticed anything peculiar. It is a testament to how conditioned Americans are to propaganda that, in five years, we have yet to have anyone who knew immediately what we were talking about.

"Well," we say, "in the book, not a single white adult resident of Dillon was willing to stand up for what was right . . ."

Then they get it.

"In the real vote, 240 people voted against the bond," someone says.

"And how many voted for?"

"Only 367."

"That means two white people out of every five voted to let the African Americans keep their homes. Where are those 240 people in the book? Which character represents the decent white people who didn't want to kick black people out of their homes?"

There isn't one.

After this comes out, there is usually uneasiness in the room. "What do you think now?" we ask.

Someone always points out that the vote doesn't change the fact that the town *was* willing to destroy the lives of fifty-eight families to put up a park.

"True, but do you feel differently about the book?"

A lot of people do feel differently. "It should have been fairer," one of the kids usually says.

"But you agree with what the author was saying," we reply. "Does it really matter if she overstated a little? It's still true, isn't it?"

Yes, it is true, but somehow it still seems to matter that the author didn't quite play fair. "So," we ask, "it's always important to think about what someone is saying, or at least the *way* they're saying it, isn't it?"

Ironically, it might have been a better book if it *wasn't* so one-sided, if the reader thought there was a chance that Freedomtown would survive, instead of knowing from the beginning that it was doomed. Evenhandedness might well have injected a greater element of suspense.

The ultimate lesson of *White Lilacs* goes beyond literary license and historical accuracy, however. Teaching kids to question opinions *they agree with* is just as important as teaching them to question those they don't.

It is rare for an author to help you out and relate exactly how they stacked the deck either for or against some of their characters. These kinds of flaws or inconsistencies in a book, as in life, are usually a good deal more subtle. We do a book in fourth grade that provides a wonderful opportunity for this sort of critical analysis.

The Giver

This best-selling award winner by Lois Lowry is set in a self-sufficient, futuristic community called The Community, which is part of a larger but unseen society. The Community, which has been made to resemble a contemporary suburban town, is benevolently governed by The Elders and populated by people who, after war and famine centuries before, relinquished individual freedom for safety and security. Personal choice has been eliminated and behavior is regulated according to a strict set of rules. Lying is forbidden, as is rudeness, lack of consideration for others, or aggressive behavior in any form. There are no books or other mass media.

To prevent conflict or want, population in the Community is strictly controlled—every set of "parents" has one boy and one girl. These parents are not biological, but are instead assigned children—there is a separate set of individuals who actually conceive and carry them. Every child grows up more or less identically, granted privileges and given responsibilities at precisely the same time. For example, every boy or girl is given a bicycle when they reach age nine. When the children reach twelve, they attend the Ceremony of Twelve (there are no individual birthday celebrations either) where each is assigned a career, based on aptitude and inclination, within which they will then function for the rest of their productive lives. When members of the Community reach an advanced but unspecified age, they stop working and are sent to the House of the Old, where they are cared for by specially trained Caretakers of the Old. At some point after that, following a solemn ceremony of celebration, they are Released and sent to Elsewhere—seemingly another Community—to live out their remaining days.

Under certain extreme circumstances, underage members of the Community may be Released as well. Anyone who chronically misbehaves (although this almost never happens), doesn't or can't follow the rules (tells lies or uses imprecise language), or questions the order of things can be Released. If twins are born, the one who weighs slightly less will be Released so that population control is not disturbed. The residents of the Community all seem to accept this regimentation without question and they also seem to be universally content. (To help them maintain this contentment, everyone takes medication to suppress their emotions, including "stirrings"—that is, sex drive—and to eliminate pain.) The only unpleasant side effect of giving up personal freedom seems to be the loss of ability to see colors.

At the Ceremony of Twelve that more or less opens the story, Jonas (no one has a last name) eagerly awaits his career assignment. Jonas, bright and sensitive, with light-colored eyes—rare in the Community—lives with kindly Dad, a Nurturer (a caregiver for infants); fair and wise Mom, who has an unspecified job in the justice ministry; and a bouncy little sister, Lily. But instead of receiving an assignment, Jonas is passed over. Panicking, feeling that he must have committed some terrible transgression, Jonas soon learns that he has been chosen for a rare honor, one which is bestowed only once in many, many years. He is to be the new Receiver of Memory.

It turns out that the Community chooses one person to be the repository of its entire history, its one link with the past. The Receiver holds not only a factual record but emotions as well. He will be able to feel pain and pleasure—in fact, he will feel all the pain and pleasure of the Community's history. He will see colors. To perform this, Jonas is instructed to stop taking medication, read books if he wishes, learn anything he wants about the inner workings of the Community, and watch anyone perform his or her job through a series of monitors placed in the work buildings. He cannot discuss what he learns with anyone, especially his friends and family.

Most of all, Jonas is now allowed to lie.

As he studies with the current Receiver, an old-before-his-time, careworn, light-eyed man, now called the Giver, Jonas is overwhelmed by the feelings and emotions he receives. (Once the Giver has transferred a specific memory or sensation to Jonas, he can no longer experience it himself.) Jonas soon feels the exhilaration of a sleigh ride but also feels the anguish of a horrible scene on a battle-field. This is all internal—there is no actual snow or carnage. Colors give him great joy and he gets a sense of love.

Jonas's sterile, artificial home life is in stark contrast to his sessions with the Giver, and he begins to wonder if the Community's decision to give up excitement, disorder, and risk for peace and security is such a good idea after all. As Jonas is wrestling with this dilemma, his father brings home an infant named Gabriel who will not sleep in the nursery and is to be given a limited time to adjust before being Released.

Jonas soon finds out, of course, that Released is a euphemism for killed. After the Ceremony of Release for an old person, for example, that person is secretly given a drug that brings on painless death. Jonas further discovers that The Giver had a daughter who had been chosen to be the Receiver ten years earlier, but she had been unable to bear the burden and demanded to be Released, choosing death to her assigned role. (When there is no Receiver, all the memories and emotions revert to the other members of the Community, bringing on enormous distress.)

Eventually, Jonas watches through a monitor as his father gently and lovingly Releases the lighter of a pair of twins by injecting some substance into his brain. When Jonas discovers that Gabriel, who will only sleep and behave properly with him, is also to be Released, he decides to run away. (There evidently *is* an Elsewhere elsewhere.) He takes Gabriel and escapes, leaving the Giver behind to help the Community cope with the flood of experiences and emotions it is about to receive.

By the time we read *The Giver*, our kids know that a made-up totalitarian society is a very popular vehicle in children's books (with *A Wrinkle in Time* and *Among the Hidden* as prominent examples) and that the setting can provide vital clues to the underlying message. As a result, we carefully examine the Community before we go on to protagonist/antagonist. We generally get the following:

- Conflict-free
- Needs are met
- Everyone has enough, but not too much.
- Everything is in its place.
- Pain free
- Fear free
- No worries
- Everyone is the same, no need to compare
- Clean
- Perfect weather
- Everyone gets the right job.
- No stress

"So what," we asked, "can possibly be wrong with that? Sounds like a pretty good place to live."

A lot of indignant hands shot up.

"But there's no freedom!" said about eight kids in unison.

"So what?" we repeated. "What do you need freedom for if you know you're going to get the perfect job and live in a comfortable house and always have plenty to eat?"

"But you can't do anything different," Hannah, a usually quiet little girl, protested vehemently.

"But why would you want to?" we countered.

The kids were confused. They understood in theory that freedom is important, but in our experience, few children understand what freedom is important *for*. The question of freedom versus security is always difficult, and there are no pat answers. When the kids have understood that, we tell them to hold that in their heads, because we'll come back to it.

Sentiment as to the identity of protagonist is usually split between Jonas and the Giver.

Jonas

- Smart
- A rebel
- Willing to lie
- Cares about Gabriel
- Asks lots of questions
- A leader

The Giver

- ▸ Old
- ▸ Willing to lie
- ▸ Afraid to leave
- ▸ Helps Jonas
- ▸ Lets his daughter die

Typically, most of the group favors Jonas as a protagonist, but without choosing between them, we move on to the antagonist. Here feelings are less strong. We usually get Jonas, the Giver, Mom, Dad, and the Elders.

With the choices this limited, we again test possible protagonist/antagonist combinations to see what the book might be about in the different cases. For example, when we asked what the action would be if the Giver were the protagonist and Jonas the antagonist, someone replied, "Maintaining a way of life." This is a good theme to explore. Does anyone have the right to tell people that they have to change the way they've chosen to live their lives? Still, "maintaining a way of life" does not really seem to be what this book is about.

If you flip the Giver and Jonas, Jonas is definitely pushing forward individual action against a group, or possibly rebelling against tyranny, but the Giver is not holding back either of these actions. If anything, the Giver shares most of the misgivings Jonas develops about how the Community functions and encourages him in his questioning. In the end, the group usually decides that the Giver seems to be too much like Jonas to be the antagonist. That leaves Dad, Mom, and the Elders. We sometimes go through each of the possibilities, but it's often better to shortcut the process a bit.

"Is there any real difference between them?" we ask. "Don't Dad, Mom, and the Elders all pretty much share the same traits? Don't they all kind of represent acceptance of the way of life in the Community?" When the group agrees that they do, we ask, "Which of them seems to embody those traits the most?"

We almost always get Dad. If we don't, we ask the group to identify the climax. It's pretty easy to see that it is the scene where Jonas sees his dad Release the little twin.

"Okay then, if Jonas is the protagonist and Dad is the antagonist, what's the conflict?"

Whether the Community is a good place.

"In other words, are the values of the Community good values? Does Jonas have that conflict with the Giver?"

No. The Giver also thinks there are things wrong. And he doesn't really hold back the action of change. He simply declines to participate himself.

It is not unusual for our kids and parents to confuse the concepts of *causing* something to happen with simply *allowing* something to happen. The Giver is perfect for illustrating a different category of character, one that appears often in a novel.

"So, what is the Giver's role?" we ask. "Any chemists in the group?"

Often, a couple of kids will raise their hands, and occasionally a parent. If not, we ask, "Anyone know what a catalyst is?"

If no one does (or at least is willing to give a definition) we say, "In chemistry, a catalyst is something that you add to other chemicals that allows them to react—change—but does not change itself. Without the catalyst you can mix those other chemicals forever and nothing at all will happen. But as soon as you add the catalyst . . . poof, you get a reaction. In this book, the Giver gives Jonas the momentum to change but does not really change himself. In fact, after Jonas leaves, he performs pretty much the same role as he did after his daughter was Released."

From there, we go back to the action. If Jonas is pushing forward questioning the values of the Community—safety and security over personal freedom—and Dad is trying to hold that back by defending a society where everyone lives honestly and honorably, no one goes hungry, no one feels pain, everyone has a job they enjoy and lives in comfort, what is this book really about? Do you really think the author is saying that getting to choose what music to listen to, say, is better than a safe and secure life?

This brings us back to the question of why freedom is precious. In our experience with *The Giver*, kids, and parents as well, have a lot of trouble with this when the Community is the standard for denial of freedom. They don't like that everyone who gets old or can't conform to the rules gets killed, of course, but they can see why the members of the Community had been driven to such drastic action. After all, their motives were pure and they were maintaining a moral and caring society, weren't they?

Or were they?

Lois Lowry's entire thesis rests on the assumption that members of the Community were basically decent people who felt they were left no choice but to live the way they did. At no point, for example, do we get any indication that Dad believed he was doing wrong in Releasing lighter twins or infants who could not conform. There was no hypocrisy in the Community. The Elders were portrayed as genuinely caring leaders who laid down rules that they believed were necessary to everyone's well-being, rules that they scrupulously followed themselves.

"Okay," we say to the group, "what if this view of the Community is wrong? What if the author has loaded the dice? What if Dad and the Elders knew they were doing wrong and there is nothing benevolent about the Community? What then? Is there any evidence for this in the book?"

"Look at people's actions," we say.

Someone will always eventually mention Dad, the disturbing scene in which he Released the twin, and that the same fate seems to await little Gabriel.

"But wasn't that his job?" we counter. "He had to Release the twin for the protection of everyone. He certainly didn't think he was doing anything wrong, did he?"

Guess not.

"What are the rules of the Community again?"

Use precise language, be considerate of others, don't lie . . .

Often, but not always, someone will say, "But Dad lied to Jonas about Release."

"Guess he broke the rules, huh? If he keeps doing that, he'll be Released."

"No," some child will protest, "he was supposed to lie about Release."

"You mean the Elders *knew* he lied?"

"They told him to lie."

"What about the Caretakers of the Old? Do they lie when they Release old people?"

Yes.

"Do the Elders know about that, too?"

Yes.

"So Dad lies because he's supposed to, the Caretakers of the Old lie because they're supposed to, and the Elders know all about it?"

At least one parent or child always falls into the trap. "Maybe they're doing it to spare the other people's feelings."

"But if the Community has adopted these rules of behavior out of necessity, because they had no other choice, and they all believe that they're doing right and protecting the lives of their citizens—most of them, anyway—*why do they need to lie about it*? If this was the way things had to be, why didn't they simply tell everyone that this was the way it had to be and make another rule? One thing the Community had no problem with was rules. *People only lie if they know they are doing something wrong.*"

The second the group understands that the notions of truth and honesty within the Community are bogus, everything about the book changes. No longer can the leaders of the Community be seen as merely misguided. They have become murderers. What is worse, every single person at the Ceremony of Twelve who is given a job that will someday require Release is willing to become a murderer as well.

Someone will always ask why this is so important.

"Because it means that the author has absolved these people of responsibility for their crimes. In this book, they're simply not supposed to know any better. But did Dad know better?"

At this point, most of the group understands that he must have known.

There is always someone who asks, "How do you know Dad knew?"

This is a vital point. If Dad is lying and knows the rules are phony, then everything about his behavior with Jonas is fake. And there's nothing whatever in the book to indicate that the author intended Dad to be faking his behavior. Even when he is alone, killing the little twin when no one is watching, he maintains his loving and caring demeanor. This is a big deal! How can he lie, breaking one of the cardinal rules of the Community, which clearly states that only the Receiver of Memory may lie, and not feel guilt, or know that he is doing something wrong? So Dad *must* know, and the Community *must* condone lying and murder.

"But how do you know that he doesn't feel guilt on the inside?" someone sometimes asks.

This is where the rule on not manufacturing evidence comes in. "Show us where it says that in the book," we reply. "Show us the passage in the text that indicates that Dad felt bad about what he had done."

There isn't one.

"So if he knew what he was doing was wrong," we go on, "if they all knew, then how would you describe the Community now?"

Needless to say, perfect weather doesn't make the new list. "Evil," however, usually does.

"What difference does it make that the Community might be evil?" we ask. "What does this have to do with Jonas? He still made the right decision to get out and save Gabriel, didn't he?"

There is usually general agreement that Jonas's choice was correct.

"What happens to the Community if Jonas leaves?"

All the memories that he got from the Giver will come back.

"But that happened once before and the Giver got them through it. And he's promised to get them through it again. So nothing will change. What is the only way things can change?"

Eventually, someone will offer, "Only if Jonas, with all his power, stays and *makes* them change."

"Yes. Jonas is no longer running away from a place where everyone believes the same things and he's different. He's running away from a place of great corruption that desperately needs him as the only one who might be able to make things better. What do you think about that?"

Once the discussion moves to whether or not Jonas should have stayed or run away, we're on to a genuine moral dilemma. After all, standing and fighting is not always the best choice, and Jonas has Gabriel to consider as well. In our discussions, however, the kids and parents have generally felt that because of the power that Jonas could exert over the Community (and there is every reason to believe that the Giver would help him), he was not taking a significant risk by staying. He most likely could have protected Gabriel as well.

Based on how the characters were constructed, the idea that Dad is a murderer, the Giver is a willing accomplice, and Jonas has run away, allowing all this to continue, doesn't seem at all to be what Lois Lowry had in mind. Still, that is what the book now seems to be about. People don't simply stumble into totalitarianism. It is either imposed on them by force or they embrace it. In the Community, it now seems to be the latter.

We always assign *The Giver* immediately after *Animal Farm* because it allows for some excellent comparisons. For example, we can ask, "Does anyone see any similarities between the Giver and Benjamin the Donkey?" What we want the kids to get to is that both the Giver and Benjamin could have tried to change things that were wrong but, for different reasons, chose not to.

Finally we ask the kids and parents to think about the choices that the two authors made as to character and setting. "George Orwell used farm animals and wrote satirically and Lois Lowry used people and wrote with realism, but which society is more real to you?"

CHAPTER 9

SONGS WITHOUT MUSIC

Poetry

Introducing elementary school children to poetry has been among our greatest pleasures. Poetry is an integral part of our literary heritage. The imagery and music of poetry feeds imagination, and the beauty of a poem will stay with a child years after he or she first reads it. When we do poetry with second and third graders, we begin in the same place the schools usually do—Shel Silverstein—and move on from there.

Before the session, we ask the kids to look through all three Shel Silverstein books—*A Light in the Attic*, *Falling Up*, and *Where the Sidewalk Ends*—and choose a poem they like. For those (very few) who have not yet experienced this poet's work, Silverstein writes comic verse, some of it wacky, some of it a little scary (by elementary school standards), and all of it accompanied by endearingly silly sketches. A typical Shel Silverstein poem runs as follows:

NOPE

I put a piece of cantaloupe
Underneath the microscope.
I saw a million strange things sleepin',
I saw a zillion weird things creepin',
I saw some green things twist and bend—
I won't eat cantaloupe again.

We have yet to meet the elementary school child, or parent, who has not loved Shel Silverstein and enjoyed combing the books for a favorite poem.

"Okay," we said. "Here's a break! No protagonist or antagonist to worry about. No wondering what the setting means, or what the conflict in a story is, or what the book is really about. No mystery. Just poetry. Easy. Everybody knows about poetry, right? So tell us . . . what exactly *is* poetry? How should we define it?"

- A kind of writing—a lot of times it rhymes.
- It is written in verses—sometimes.
- It is a time when you want to use fewer words to say a lot.
- It has a rhythm.
- It is written in a kind of pattern, not the way you usually write.
- Poetry isn't written like a story.
- It can sometimes tell a story, though.
- It's a very quiet way of expressing great emotion. (A mom.)

- There are different types of poetry, like haikus.
- The words are chosen much more carefully, and therefore mean more.
- It is usually to express an opinion of the world.
- It makes use of similes and metaphors. (A dad.)

"Uh-huh," we say. "Mind if we give it a try?"

- A song without music
- A painting in words
- The highest form of written expression
- Truth

"No truth, no poetry," we said. "A string of beautiful words is not poetry. It has to say something, something universal, a truth we all recognize. Robert Frost said a poem 'begins in delight and ends in wisdom,' and that's what we think he meant. And it has to bring out that truth by both painting a picture and composing a song, just with words, and with the most economical number of words. A very, very, very difficult thing to do, which is why poetry is usually considered the highest form of written expression."

Once we got a sort of working definition, we moved on to the poet and his or her role in our society.

"Do we need poems or poets? Are they really necessary? It's not like a doctor, right? We need doctors for when we get sick. Who do you think earns more money, a doctor or a poet?"

Adam's hand shot up. Adam was the boy who loved the

blood-drinking in *Charlotte's Web*. "The poet earns more money, because you have to buy the book," he said. (If that were only true, we thought.)

"As opposed to going to the doctor. When you go to the doctor it's free, right?"

"Right!" said Adam.

"Wrong," we said. "It costs money every time you visit the doctor. Doctors make *a lot* more money than poets. Poets make almost no money. Poets have to *marry* doctors in order to make money."

"Oh," Adam grunted, but he looked unconvinced.

"So let's go back to the original question: What do poets do for people?"

- Helps you see the truth
- Helps you see things differently
- Entertains people
- Soothes a restless spirit (that same mom again)
- When things get hard it is a place to go to and maybe get some answers.
- Reflects back how we are feeling
- Helps us to slow down (a dad)

"There's something else the poet does for people. Can anyone guess?"

No one could, so we resorted to the ever-trusty hangman.

_ _ _ _ _ _ _ (INSPIRE)

"What does that mean, to 'inspire' someone?"

"You make them feel better," offered Julie.

"You give them the courage to try harder," added Ben's mom.

"Exactly," we said. "Now let's turn to Shel Silverstein's work. What kind of poetry does he write? What are his poems like?"

"They're silly," said Samantha.

"They're fiction," noted Ben, after a whispered conference with his mother. "They're all made up."

"You mean exaggerated."

"Yes."

"Who are they about, mostly? Parents or kids?"

"Kids."

"Yes, they're about kids. But here's the funny thing. Shel Silverstein never married and raised a family. He didn't live with a houseful of kids. So how did he come to write poems that show so much knowledge of who kids are and what they like?"

"He must have paid attention to other people's kids," said Courtney's mom.

"He observed," said Joe's dad.

"Maybe he remembered from when he was a kid," said Brittany.

This is a very important point. We always want to get across to the kids how much their world expands when they pay attention. So we told them how Shel Silverstein observed, very carefully, always paid attention, even from the time he was little. He watched and he remembered.

It's a little sad, but maybe that's something else a poet

does for us—takes the time to observe when the rest of us are too busy. Poets watch and think about what they've seen and then show us in poems all the stuff we've missed by not really paying attention.

After that, we let the kids read the poems they had picked. It is a good exercise in itself to stand up in front of a group and read a poem. We asked the kids what they liked about each poem, and usually they said that they chose it because it was funny.

Then we read a poem from *A Light in the Attic*.

HOW MANY, HOW MUCH

How many slams in an old screen door?
Depends how loud you shut it.
How many slices in a bread?
Depends how thin you cut it.
How much good inside a day?
Depends how good you live 'em.
How much love inside a friend?
Depends how much you give 'em.

This is an excellent poem to take apart and use as an example of the manner in which poetry is constructed. "Sometimes," we said, "not always, a poem moves from a concrete, objective observation to something much more subjective, not so easy to define. Objective means that it is something we can measure. We can take Adam here and measure him with a ruler and find out how tall he is. That's an objective truth. But if we say 'Adam is the best boy in the whole world,' is there any way to objectively measure that?" (Adam insisted that there was.) "Can we take out a ruler and measure his bestness? No. Saying Adam is the best boy in the whole world is subjective. It is someone's opinion, the kind of thing people can argue about. How do we measure bestness? We can't."

The poem begins with an objective observation. "How many slams in an old screen door? / Depends how loud you shut it."

A child can envision an old screen door, just kind of hanging on its hinges, and then slamming it. He or she could *objectively* count the number of slams until the door fell off. Same with the next line, "How many slices in a bread? / Depends how thin you cut it." Kids could conceivably take a loaf of bread, slice it, and then count the slices. If they wanted to slice it thinner, they could slice each slice. (Don't actually let them try this.) But they *could* count the sliced slices.

But in the next line, it starts to get a little trickier. How is it possible to measure how much good there is inside a day?

The move from objective to subjective is difficult. Ben suggested counting all the good things that happened that day. We responded that what is good to one person isn't necessarily good to another. We don't really have a way to *measure* goodness.

In fact, the poem has changed with this line. It has gone from a tangible image to something deeper and more significant. This is called "opening up." And then, of course, the next line—"How much love inside a friend? / Depends how much you give 'em"—is much the same. You have to give of yourself to get the most out of your life and your friends, and the more you give, the more you will receive.

It was here that the group understood that a poem is also a kind of mystery. Once again, there was a hidden truth to be found, only this time the text was shorter and the clues more obscure. Instead of studying a character, or an incident in a plot, here they had to think hard about the words themselves.

When they got that, we moved on to Robert Frost. Sometimes a writer is just as interesting as his writing, and Frost is worth taking some time with. In addition, Robert Frost's life had a direct bearing on the meanings imbedded in his poems, and knowing something about him makes his poetry richer. We sketched his life like this:

"Robert Frost was one of the greatest American poets. He won the Pulitzer Prize for poetry four times—no one else has ever done that. He wrote and recited a poem at the inauguration of President John F. Kennedy. In his lifetime he traveled across the country teaching and reading poetry. He was one of the most beloved and respected Americans of his time.

"But he didn't start out that way. It was very hard for him. He was born in California, which is funny, because today he is always identified with New England. His father died when he was a boy and his mother moved to Massachusetts to be near his father's family. He grew up poor even though his grandfather was well-off. He did very well in school and went to college for a semester but dropped out. He wanted to be a poet, but it was very hard to earn a living writing poems. He got sick and his doctor advised him to live a more outdoor life, so he and his wife and children went to live on a farm in New England.

"For seven years, Robert Frost raised chickens. It was very hard work—the family survived by growing its own food. But this experience was crucial to Frost's development as a poet, because during those years of farming, he spent a great deal of time reading, observing nature, and just listening—listening to everyday sounds that pass us by, like the sound of a plow, or the way his next-door neighbors talked, or the wind at night during a storm. And at the end of that period, he started to write his poems. He didn't tell anyone, though. His neighbors already thought he was a terrible farmer and supported by his grandfather, and he knew that they would look down their noses at him even more if they thought he was doing something so silly. He said he'd rather wear a millstone around his neck than confess to them that he was a poet.

"He took his poems to New York, to publishers, but they didn't buy them. He didn't look like a poet to them either. They looked at his boots and saw mud on them, and they turned him down.

"Then his grandfather died and left him some money and he took his whole family to England. There, an English publisher gave him his first chance by publishing a book of his poems. It was only after the book came out in England that an American publisher agreed to publish his poetry. So one of the greatest American poets had to get published in England before anyone here would recognize his talent! It was only after his English trip that he began to get noticed, and finally became famous.

"Most of his best work is rooted in those years of farming in New England. Let's look at one of his poems:

NOTHING GOLD CAN STAY

Nature's first green is gold,
Her hardest hue to hold.
Her early leaf's a flower;
But only so an hour.
Then leaf subsides to leaf.
So Eden sank to grief,
So dawn goes down to day.
Nothing gold can stay.

This is a great poem to start with because it is short, which means it will hold any child's attention when you go through it line by line. Unlike in a story, the clues in a poem are much more compressed, each line crucial to what is coming next, one image building upon another. "Nature's first green is gold," we read. "What does *that* mean?"

No hands were raised.

"Let's think about it. Nature's first green. When is nature—the outside—first green?"

"Could he mean spring?" asked Samantha.

"Yes! Exactly. Think back to what the outside looks like when it first gets to be spring. Can anyone describe the beginning of spring?"

"The snow melts."

"It gets warmer."

"The grass gets green."

"There are leaves on the trees."

"And flowers."

"Right," we said. "In fact, the whole world looks like somebody took a paintbrush and painted the sky blue, the grass green, and the daffodils yellow, doesn't it? Pay attention the next time it is spring and really look around at the grass and the trees and the flowers and you'll see this is so. So nature's first green refers to spring. Then what does Frost mean when he says it's gold? He said spring is green, not gold, right?"

The kids understood that, in this line, gold meant something precious, and that Frost used the concept of gold in place of the word *precious*. So, "Nature's first green is gold" meant that the first green of spring was precious. In the next line, "Her hardest hue to hold," the kids didn't know that "hue" means a shade of color, but once we told them, they figured out what the line meant.

"What's hard to hold?"

"A puppy."

"A baby."

"Something hot."

"Something cold."

"A fish!" exclaimed Joe, in the tone of one who could claim firsthand experience.

"Yes. Robert Frost is saying that that very first green of spring is hard to hold—like a fish—you can't keep it around very long. The very first buds of leaves on the trees are a different shade of green than the green of leaves in summer. They are a little brighter—we even call it spring green. Then he talks about the buds. He says, 'Her early leaf's a flower; / But only so an hour. / Then leaf subsides to leaf.' "

We went on to explain that the buds on the trees really do look like little flowers—they make us happy when we look at them. But they are only buds a very short time. More than an hour—he's using that phrase figuratively to mean a short time—but not more than a few days, possibly a week. Then, when he says, "leaf subsides to leaf," it means that the delicate little buds open and grow and become regular leaves. Still pretty, still nice to look at, but not the same. Not the same color green, not the same shape. He's saying you have to really look at the beauty of those first buds of spring before they give way to something else— they are precious.

Kids never get the next line, but it's not too hard to explain.

" 'So Eden sank to grief' refers to the Garden of Eden. Does anyone know the story of Adam and Eve?"

Most elementary school children know this story. Eden was a perfect place, special, like the buds of early spring. Adam and Eve didn't want to leave. That's what Frost meant when he said Eden sank to grief. It was precious and they had to leave and that was the reason for their grief. This is where the poem opens up. It's not just about spring anymore. It's about something deeper.

"So dawn goes down to day" is next. Anyone who has ever seen a sunrise knows how beautiful it is, filled with amazing colors. Then the sun comes up and the colors fade. Day is nice, but not quite as beautiful as dawn. Dawn is something else that is precious, new, and beautiful but only for a short time.

Then finally, the last line says, "Nothing gold can stay." Beauty like the first buds of spring, the Garden of Eden, and dawn are like gold, precious, but they are fleeting. We cannot hold on to them and see them whenever we want.

These moments of beauty are all around us. We asked if anyone ever saw a perfect dive at the Olympics. It's so beautiful, and it is over so quickly. Did anyone see Sarah Hughes skate her long program at the 2002 Winter Olympics? It was breathtaking. She didn't think she had a chance so she just went out there and skated her heart out and it was so incredibly beautiful that they gave her the gold medal for it.

"Are there any moments you can think of that were golden for you? A time that was really special?"

"My birthday party."

"When I rode my bike for the first time."

"When I first danced in the *Nutcracker*."

"The first time I saw my daughter," said Courtney's mom.

The group intuitively understood that, in this poem, Robert Frost was also saying that many of these precious moments are at the beginning of things, and that is what makes them so fleeting. Spring is when life reawakens at the beginning of each year, dawn is the beginning of each day, and Eden was at the beginning of man's spiritual journey. Perhaps it is part of their beauty that they don't stay. You have to appreciate them while they're here.

We like to do another Robert Frost poem after this, one that for us contains about the most important message there is.

THE ROAD NOT TAKEN

Two roads diverged in a yellow wood,
And sorry I could not travel both
And be one traveler, long I stood
And looked down one as far as I could
To where it bent in the undergrowth;

Then took the other, as just as fair,
And having perhaps the better claim,
Because it was grassy and wanted wear;
Though as for that the passing there
Had worn them really about the same,

And both that morning equally lay
In leaves no step had trodden black.
Oh, I kept the first for another day!
Yet knowing how way leads on to way,
I doubted if I should ever come back.

I shall be telling this with a sigh
Somewhere ages and ages hence:
Two roads diverged in a wood, and I—
I took the one less traveled by,
And that has made all the difference.

We do the same thing with this poem as we did with "Nothing Gold Can Stay" and "How Many, How Much"—we go through it line by line.

" 'Two roads diverged in a yellow wood.' What is a yellow wood?" we asked.

"There are yellow flowers on the ground?"

"Not yellow flowers. When else are the woods yellow? Any particular time of year?"

"Fall?"

"Right. If you look around at the trees in fall the leaves are turning red and orange and yellow. Using 'yellow wood' is a way to describe the woods in fall. So 'Two roads diverged in a yellow wood'—diverged means parted, went in separate directions—means what?"

"That there are two roads going in different directions in the woods in fall."

"Good. Let's go to the next two lines: 'And sorry I could not travel both / And be one traveler.' What does that mean?" To cement the image, we perform a demonstration.

"Ben, will you come up front here for a moment, please?" One of us held Ben by the shoulders. "Okay, Ben, here you are walking in the woods in autumn, and suddenly, the path you're taking splits into two roads. One goes this way"—we point in one direction—"and one goes the other. Can you take both?"

"No," said Ben.

"So how do you decide which road to take? How does the poet decide? What does the next line say?"

"Long I stood / And looked down one as far as I could / To where it bent in the undergrowth."

"So what does that mean he does?"

"He looks down one path as far as he can."

"Yes. So, Ben, look down that path as far as you can." Ben pretended to look in one direction. "But you can't see all the way, can you? Robert Frost says it bends, and then there are too many bushes and stuff—that's undergrowth—to really tell which way it goes, or how easy or difficult a path it is, right? So that's one road. What does he say next?"

"Then took the other, as just as fair / And having perhaps the better claim, / Because it was grassy and wanted wear."

"It means he took the other path."

"Yes, he takes the other path. But why? He tells us."

There were two reasons. The first, because it was "just as fair," meant it looked just as inviting or attractive. The second, "it had a better claim," meant it was somehow more deserving of his walking there.

"Because it was grassy, nicer to walk on," said Courtney.

"That's right," we said, "but Frost also said that it wanted wear. He meant that it wasn't all trampled. Evidently, not many people took that road because it didn't look used. 'Wanted wear' means unused. So, on what did he base his decision?"

"He took the path most people don't use," said Julie.

"Why would someone take a road that other people

avoid?" we asked. "Isn't that foolish? After all, there must have been a reason people took the popular way. Isn't it scary to go someplace strange? And yet the man who wrote this poem says to do exactly that—to go the way other people don't.

"The poet says some more about the path. 'Though as for that the passing there / Had worn them really about the same / And both that morning equally lay / In leaves no step had trodden black.' He says on that day, right at the junction—the crossroads where Ben is standing, looking down, trying to decide—the paths look like no one had used either.

"The next line is, 'Oh, I kept the first for another day! / Yet knowing how way leads on to way / I doubted if I should ever come back.' "

"He's going to take the first path another day," said Adam.

"But will he?" we replied. "It seems that the poet knows that it is unlikely he'll ever be back at this exact spot again. He may *want* to experience both paths, but he's got to make a definite choice. And he does. He takes the second path."

This is where the poem opens up:

> I shall be telling this with a sigh
> Somewhere ages and ages hence:
> Two roads diverged in a wood, and I—
> I took the one less traveled by,
> And that has made all the difference.

Robert Frost is talking about the future, of course. A long time from now, "ages and ages hence," he'll sigh and tell someone that he once had a choice between two paths and he took the one less traveled by.

" 'And that has made all the difference.' The difference in what?" we asked the kids. "Do you think he's still talking about those two paths in the wood?"

No.

"What then?"

"He's talking about his life," said Julie's mom.

"So Robert Frost is saying that it was making the difficult choice, taking the path everyone else didn't, that made all the difference? I guess this was a warning?"

"No!!!"

"You mean he meant it in a good way, an encouraging way? That people *should* take the riskier choice, *should* make decisions other people might not agree with, that in the end taking the road less traveled might lead to a better place than the road everyone else takes?"

Fervent agreement.

"Could this be another example of following your dreams, like in *Mr. Popper's Penguins*?"

Maybe.

"Did Robert Frost practice what he preached? Did *he* take the road less traveled?"

Yes.

"How?"

"He became a poet," said Samantha.

"Yes! That was definitely a road less traveled. Do lots

of people become poets? Do you think it is a difficult decision to become a poet? Remember what we said about
poets in the beginning. They don't make a lot of money.
No job security, no health care. [That's for the parents.]
Robert Frost didn't even want to let his neighbors in New
Hampshire know that he wrote poetry. He thought they'd
make fun of him. Remember how hard it was for him to
become a poet! Remember those New York publishers
rejecting him because he had mud on his shoes! But wait
a minute, is Robert Frost saying that everyone should be a
poet, that everyone should *always* take the road less traveled?"

"No. He's saying that it was right for him," said Adam's
dad.

"Yes. He is telling us to choose what is right for us.
When you grow up, you'll face the same sort of decisions.
You'll stand at the edge of a path and try to figure out
where it will lead—imagine what your life will be like—but
you won't know for sure. But do you think Robert Frost
was only talking about picking a career, or was he trying to
get at something more important, like learning to think for
yourself?"

Everyone reaches crossroads, we say, and not just for
big things. Other people will often try to convince you to
take the safe path, but the safe path isn't always so safe.
Kids might try to tell you that it's more important to be
popular than nice, or it is fun to tease that new kid who
dresses differently or speaks with an accent. Every time
you have to decide what to do, it is another crossroads. If

you get too much in the habit of going the way everyone else goes, it becomes almost impossible to choose the road less traveled. But if you get used to thinking for yourself, you will be able to choose what is best for you.

And that might make all the difference.

A BOOK FOR PRACTICE

We love the 1961 classic *Phantom Tollbooth* by
Norton Juster. Many parents will remember it from
their own childhoods. We do it early, in third grade, in
order to introduce kids to the language, wit, and easy intelligence of this book as soon as possible. It is a testament to
the power of *The Phantom Tollbooth* that it is equally appealing to both eight-year-olds and their parents.

The Phantom Tollbooth

Milo is a boy who rushes about in his own life, never really
seeing anything. He has no particular interests and is bored
most of the time. One day, he comes home from school and
finds a large box in his bedroom. The box contains a cardboard tollbooth and a map of a country called "The Kingdom of Wisdom," which Milo has never heard of. He
assembles the tollbooth, randomly chooses a destination

off the map, hops into his toy automobile, deposits a coin in the appropriate slot and lo and behold, he finds himself driving along on a real road in this strange land.

Milo discovers that the Kingdom of Wisdom is, at the moment, in a state of confusion, owing to the absence of two princesses, Rhyme and Reason. These two proponents of fairness and reasonableness were banished to the Castle in the Air for failing to resolve an argument—over whether words or numbers were more important—to the satisfaction of their brothers, King Azaz the Unabridged, from the Kingdom of Dictionopolis, and the Mathemagician, from the Kingdom of Digitopolis. (The princesses had decided that words and numbers were of equal importance.) The brothers have since regretted their decision, and Milo, along with a watchdog named Tock (whose upper body is comprised of a clock that goes tick, tick, tick) and the Humbug (a large insect much given to boasting and pretending to know more than he does) are enlisted to undertake the perilous journey to the Castle in the Air. To rescue the princesses, they must outsmart the Demons of Ignorance who jealously guard the entrance.

After many adventures involving words, numbers, music, sound, color, and perspective, Milo, Tock, and the Humbug do indeed succeed in freeing the princesses. Milo returns home expecting to use the tollbooth again, but it has vanished. At first, Milo is disappointed, but then he realizes that there is so much to do at home, so much to learn and see, that he can be happy right there.

The Phantom Tollbooth is remarkably clever. Where else can one find an author who can imagine Milo and

Tock and a gaggle of king's advisers in a buggy pulled with no visible means of locomotion, have Milo ask, "But how will it go?" and have one of the advisers reply, "Shh! For it goes without saying," and then, sure enough, as soon as everyone is quiet, have the cart move quickly through the streets?

Whenever we do this book, we take a big dictionary, put it on a chair in the front of the room, and stick a cardboard sign on it that says: "WELCOME TO DICTIONOPOLIS."

The trick in doing *The Phantom Tollbooth* is to treat it as a narrative and let the wordplay flow from the discussion. We begin with the standard question, "So what is this book really about?" Some of the answers we got back were:

- ▸ Working hard
- ▸ It is a good thing to study many different things and use them.
- ▸ You can do a lot of things in just a little time.
- ▸ Everything has a story and it pays to look for it.
- ▸ The joy of simply learning
- ▸ Learning is fun.
- ▸ Curiosity is important.
- ▸ It is good to have friends you can trust.
- ▸ Learn from your mistakes.
- ▸ You shouldn't always be bored or think everything is boring.
- ▸ You should always have something to do.

When we asked our third graders to describe the setting, they found it irresistible not to mention the various geographic locations in the Kingdom of Wisdom.

- The Lands Beyond
- The Sea of Knowledge
- The Mountains of Ignorance
- Dictionopolis
- Conclusions
- The Doldrums
- Digitopolis
- The Valley of Sound
- The Foothills of Confusion
- The Castle in the Air
- The Forest of Sight
- Expectations
- The Kingdom of Wisdom
- Point of View

"What kind of a book is this, fiction or nonfiction?" we asked.

"Fiction."

"Does that mean it is real or made up?"

"Made up."

"Does anyone know what kind of book this is? What genre?"

We had already explained genre. "Fantasy," said Evan.

"Fairy tale," said Christina. She had new hoop earrings on.

"But what interesting names these places have for a fantasy. What do you think they mean? Is this the same kind of fantasy as, say, *Snow White* or *Cinderella*? Why name a place wisdom, or ignorance, or confusion?"

"Well, it's an allegory," said Will's mom.

"What's an allegory?"

"I'm not exactly sure," she admitted. (We hadn't done allegory yet.)

"Welcome to Dictionopolis," we said, and pointed to the dictionary.

Kids love it when a mom or dad has to go to the dictionary to look something up.

"Allegory, noun, narrative description of a subject under guise of another suggestively similar; emblem," Will's mom read. "A narrative that serves as an extended metaphor."

"What does *that* mean?" Nicole asked.

"Pretending to talk about one thing but really talking about something else. Does that sound like this book? Could the description of The Lands Beyond represent something other than just fantasy?"

Maybe.

"Ever see one of those fun house mirrors at a carnival?" we asked. "Where you look at yourself and you are suddenly much wider or much thinner? Much shorter or much taller? It's still you, but from a different perspective, yes? Does that kind of sound like what's going on in the setting of this book?"

Although Milo is prominent, we've always been surprised at the number of other characters kids and parents come up with for protagonist.

- Milo
- Tock
- Azaz
- The Humbug
- The Phantom Tollbooth
- Rhyme and Reason
- The Mathemagician

Since the majority favored Milo, we began there. "What was the character of Milo like at the very beginning of the book?"

- Used to have a bored and dumb life
- Had a lot of stuff he didn't use
- Walked the same way every day
- Was confused—when he was in he wanted to be out, when out wanted to be in
- Didn't use his time well
- Never wants to be where he is
- Always thinks he's in the wrong place at the wrong time

"How does the author sum up Milo's problem? Can anyone find it in the book?"

" 'And, since no one bothered to explain otherwise, he regarded the process of seeking knowledge as the greatest waste of time of all,' " read Robert.

"Okay, be honest. How many of you have thought that yourselves, or know kids who think that way?"

"Well," said Anna, "sometimes school is boring, but you *do* learn a lot."

"But it's not really fun," said Will glumly.

"You don't do much on half days," Christina observed.

"But you-need-school-to-get-good-grades-to-go-to-college-to-get-a-good-job-to-make-lots-of-money," said Nicole all in a rush, repeating a familiar refrain.

"Is that so? Is that why we learn? Maybe we should hold that thought and come back to it," we said. "Is Milo the same at the end of the book as he is at the beginning?"

No. He changes.

"How does he change?"

"He likes learning at the end of the book," Evan's father pointed out. "He thinks learning is fun at the end of the book."

"So Milo takes a journey, right? He gets into his car and drives around and has all of these adventures and meets new people and hears different points of view. And from that, you're saying he changes? Is it possible to change on the inside by having these sorts of adventures? And is the journey just physical, just in the car? Or is there another kind of journey he's taking?" These are big words for third graders, so we often resort to hangman, and we give them a start.

S _ _ _ _ _ _ _ _ (SPIRITUAL)

I _ _ _ _ _ _ _ _ _ _ (INTELLECTUAL)

"What does *that* mean?" Will asked when the blanks were filled in.

"Let's figure it out. Intellectual. It's like your intelligence. Where do you keep your intelligence?"

"In your brain."

"Right. So Milo takes an intellectual journey because he uses his intelligence and he changes that way. But he changes another way, too. Is he happy at the beginning of the book?"

"No!"

"Is he happy at the end?"

"Yes!"

"That's the spiritual journey. What's your spirit?"

"Uhh . . . inside you?" asked Anna.

"In your heart?" asked a mom.

"It's definitely something on the inside, isn't it? Something that you can feel. You can feel when your spirits are up and when they are down. You can tell when you are unhappy or bored. If Milo takes this journey and he's unhappy and bored at the beginning and happy and excited at the end, what is the author saying caused this?"

"His adventures. They were fun," said Robert.

"And they were fun because . . . ?"

"He learned he could do stuff," said Evan.

"Yes. And from learning, using his brain, he changed his spirit, didn't he? Is this because he's going to go out now and get good grades and go to a good college so he can get a good job and earn lots of money? Or is it because the act of learning all by itself is what is rewarding? Was *that* where the fun was?"

We dealt with other possible protagonists by asking the kids if a character had changed over the course of the book. The kids saw quickly that Tock, for example, did not change very much at all. He was literally a watchdog from beginning to end; his job was to see that people did not waste time.

Rhyme and Reason, however, were more plausible.

- They help in arguments.
- They settle things fairly.
- They are the adopted daughters of Wisdom.
- Without them there's chaos.
- Things are becoming worse.
- They have been banished to the Castle in the Air.

"What is Milo doing in this book?" we asked.

"Trying to save the princesses."

"Isn't the main goal in the story to return Rhyme and Reason to the Kingdom of Wisdom?"

The kids agreed it was.

"Can Rhyme and Reason be the protagonists if the goal is to rescue them? Do they do anything to help themselves or do they just wait for someone to rescue them?"

"They just wait."

"Do protagonists usually just sit there? Aren't protagonists supposed to be more active than that?" we asked.

Probably, the group agreed.

With the princesses ruled out, the group opted for Milo as protagonist. Antagonist, however, was a much more difficult choice. We got:

- The demons from the Mountains of Ignorance
- The Humbug
- Rhyme and Reason
- Azaz and the Mathemagician

"What does Humbug mean?" we asked.

"Something like a bug that hums?" asked Christina.

We pointed to the dictionary. "Welcome to Dictionopolis."

"Fraud, sham, deception, imposter," read Christina.

"So the Humbug is one who deceives or lies about who he is. That's an imposter. Does that describe the character?"

"The Humbug always pretends to know something even when he doesn't."

"He wasn't brave. He always tried to agree with everybody."

"He always tried to take credit for stuff he doesn't do."

"But if the goal is to rescue the princesses, if that's the key to the action," we asked, "is he holding back that action?"

"No. He started it."

"Yes, he did, didn't he? He convinced Azaz to send Milo. And, although he's never a big help, just having another body there sometimes makes Milo and Tock feel better, doesn't it?"

So the Humbug can't really be the antagonist.

Rhyme and Reason were also ruled out immediately. They weren't trying to hold back their own rescue. Azaz and the Mathemagician couldn't be the antagonists either, because they gave Milo gifts to help him against the demons. That left only the Demons from the Mountains of Ignorance. Who were they? (When we wrote these down for the group, we underlined the key words.)

- The Demon of *Insincerity*
- The Senses Taker (*steals senses*. "Television!" exclaimed Robert's mom in abrupt recognition.)
- The Terrible Trivium (*mindless tasks*)
- The Triple Demons of *Compromise*
- The Gelatinous Giant (*fear, insecurity, never wanting to rock the boat or change*)
- The Gross *Exaggeration*
- The Threadbare *Excuse*
- The Horrible Hopping *Hindsight*
- The Everpresent Word Snatcher (*interruption*. "He's only a nuisance, not a real demon," Nicole remarked.)
- The Gorgons of *Hate* and *Malice*
- The Overbearing *Know-It-All*

"What are all these demons, anyway? Aren't they just the obstacles to learning, to not trying? Compromise, fear, excuses, mindless tasks—aren't they just ways to stop you from becoming an educated, more developed person? Aren't these really the weapons of ignorance—hate, malice, know-it-alls? Not just clever and entertaining made-up entities, but real-life demons that we see every day?" we asked. (And which the kids, the real Milos, have to be on the alert for.)

"These demons seem pretty tough. How does Milo trick them? What protection does he have?"

He has his gifts.

"Name them."

The first gift is the box of words Milo got from Azaz, who tells him why they are so important. " 'In this box are all the words I know,' " read Evan. " 'Most of them you will never need, some you will use constantly, but with them you may ask all the questions which have never been answered and answer all the questions which have never been asked. All the great books of the past and all the ones to come are made with these words. With them there is no obstacle you cannot overcome.' "

"Wouldn't it be nice to receive a gift like that?" we asked.

"Yes."

"Well, there it is," we said, pointing at the dictionary.

From Point-of-View, Milo got a telescope. "So you see, the way you see things depends a great deal on where you look at them from." From the Soundkeeper he received a box of sounds, including the sound of laughter. In Digitopolis, Milo got a staff shaped like a pencil, to work out problems. "For one of the nicest things about mathematics, or anything else you might care to learn," said one of the characters, "is that many of the things which can never be, often are . . . it's very much like your trying to reach Infinity . . . just because you can never reach it doesn't mean that it's not worth looking for."

As Rhyme and Reason add, "You must never feel badly about making mistakes . . . as long as you take the trouble to learn from them. For you often learn more by being wrong for the right reasons than you do by being right for the wrong reasons."

"In the book, after Milo rescues Rhyme and Reason, there's a big party and Azaz and the Mathemagician tell him something they refused to reveal before he left," we said. "Who remembers what that was?"

"That it was impossible."

"So how did Milo accomplish the impossible?"

"He just did it."

"Can you know what is impossible before you try? Think of all the things we take for granted today—television, computers, telephones, airplane travel—what do you think people who lived a thousand years ago would have said about a rocket to Mars?"

"That it was impossible," acknowledged Evan's dad.

All of our technological advances, our moon shots, our life-saving drugs, and even those cool computer programs that kids like so much, all of them started very simply, with a pencil and an idea—the same gifts Milo was given. *The Phantom Tollbooth* asks kids not to be afraid to try, no matter how difficult the task seems, because the great joy of life springs from the effort, the journey, and not the result.

CHAPTER 11

ANOTHER BOOK FOR PRACTICE

We always begin our fourth-grade groups with another Newbery Award winner, *The View from Saturday* by E. L. Konigsburg. While the story is engaging and there are a number of issues to discuss, the principal reason we choose it is that the underlying message, which has to do with civility, kindness, and quiet courage, is one that no elementary school child should miss.

The View from Saturday

This is the story of four sixth-grade misfits from the small upstate New York town of Epiphany who band together and are then recruited by a misfit teacher to represent their school in the statewide Academic Bowl. Each of the four has a different reason for being set apart. The teacher, Mrs. Eva Marie Olinski, is in a wheelchair as a result of a horrible automobile accident in which her husband was killed, and has just returned to teaching after a ten-year absence.

Three of the four children are linked by circumstance but are not friends. Annoying Noah Gershon, a dentist's son, thinks of himself as a walking encyclopedia and has adopted a computerlike way of speaking. His father has recently employed Nadia Diamondstein's mother, who has divorced Nadia's accountant father and moved to New York from Florida. While on summer vacation back in Florida, Nadia, moody and withdrawn after the divorce, is forced to spend time with Ethan Potter, who lives in the shadow of an accomplished older brother, and whose grandmother Margaret Draper, a former principal at the Epiphany middle school, has recently married Nadia's grandfather Izzie. (Got that?) Into this mix is thrown the fourth child, Julian Singh, a boy from India whose mother died when he was young and whose father, a former chef on a cruise ship, has just bought a sprawling, run-down house in Epiphany, which he intends to convert into a bed-and-breakfast.

Julian, with his dark skin, English accent, Bermuda shorts and kneesocks, is, of course, the most obvious outsider and is immediately singled out and tormented by another boy in Mrs. Olinski's class, a ringleader named Hamilton Knapp. Julian refuses to respond to Ham's cruelty and doggedly continues to conduct himself with quiet dignity, which only infuriates his tormenters that much more. Ham, while very bright, is also vicious and takes every occasion to strike out not just at Julian but at anyone he perceives to be weak (although, like most bullies, he will do nothing alone). When Mrs. Olinski is out of the room, he and his crony, Michael Froelich, write "cripple" on the blackboard.

Mrs. Olinski is beset on all sides. In addition to having to figure out how to neutralize the bullies in her class, she has to fend off an administration that is populated by self-satisfied morons. For example, after receiving a lecture on the importance of multiculturalism, she is chastised by the school superintendent for describing her new student as an "Indian."

"We call them Native Americans," the superintendent noted.

"Not this one."

"Mrs. Olinski," the superintendent asked, "would you like it if people called you a cripple?"

(The rest of the educational crew is no better. At the previous year's Academic Bowl district championship, the deputy superintendent of schools pronounced the name Pope John Paul II as "Pope John Paul Eye Eye.")

But mostly, Mrs. Olinski is struggling with life in a wheelchair. Her husband is gone; she will never have children of her own. When Ethan's grandmother gives him a big hug, Mrs. Olinski feels such jealousy that she can barely contain herself.

Soon after the beginning of the term, Julian sneaks cryptic messages to Noah, Nadia, and Ethan, each with an *Alice in Wonderland* reference that Julian, who has observed each of the other kids carefully, knows they will recognize. The invitations are for a Saturday tea at his father's inn, an unusual activity to say the least for a group of American middle schoolers. Nonetheless, all three decide to attend and, with Julian as the glue, find that despite their differences, they are a whole greater than the sum of their parts. They begin to meet every Saturday for tea.

At almost the same time, Mrs. Olinski is asked to choose a four-person team for the Academic Bowl. Noah, Nadia, and Ethan are obvious choices and, by a process she cannot explain, she decides to make Julian the fourth. The group names itself "the Souls," and proceeds to defeat not only all the teams in their own grade, but the seventh-, and then the eighth-grade teams as well.

Although the Souls' success in the Academic Bowl is at the forefront of the story, *The View from Saturday* covers a good deal of other ground as well. Ginger, Nadia's dog ("a genius," as Nadia assures everyone), lands the role of Sandy in the school play, *Annie*, with Michael Froelich's dog as understudy. To punish Nadia, Hamilton Knapp attempts to feed Ginger dog treats laced with a laxative just before the performance. Julian discovers the plot at the very last minute and, using wit and intelligence rather than anger or brawn, foils Hamilton's scheme.

In the end, the Souls win the statewide Bowl and many of the students (including, significantly, Michael Froelich) come to see the members of the team not as outcast nerds but rather as four people whom they are proud to have represent them and their school.

Because this book has so many layers and characters, and begins so disjointedly (the first four chapters deal with the intertwining backgrounds of the Souls) there is always a great deal of confusion over just who the author intended as the book's protagonist and antagonist. This confusion is reflected in the number of characters that make the list of potential nominees for each category. In one of our groups, when we asked who might be the protagonist and who might be the antagonist, we got back the following:

Protagonist	*Antagonist*
► Julian	► Hamilton Knapp
► Mrs. Olinski	► Michael Froelich
► Nadia	► Mrs. Olinski
► Ethan	► Ethan
► The Souls	► The Souls
► Mr. Singh (Julian's father)	► Julian
	► The district superintendent

We have learned not to be discouraged when we get back lists like this. We've had groups that nominated nearly every character in this book as protagonist, including Nadia's grandmother Mrs. Draper, who appears in maybe ten pages altogether, and even Hamilton Knapp. It doesn't mean that the group doesn't understand the concept of protagonist. It simply means that there is so much going on in this book that it is difficult to single out the most important theme and to find the character that best represents that theme.

In order to narrow the field a bit, we ask for short nominating speeches in which each person who chose a character specifies what action they believe their nominee is pushing forward or holding back. For example, a parent who nominated Mrs. Olinski as protagonist said that the action she was pushing forward was "real education" (against, for example, the district superintendent's antagonist who was trying to hold learning back).

If the action that is described for a character seems trivial, or off the point, or even simply wrong, it is easy to then take him or her off the list. Another effective way to eliminate a minor character from consideration as protagonist or antagonist is by using the concept of "most." For example, when Michael Froelich is nominated for antagonist and we ask the group to list his traits, we get a list that is similar to that for Hamilton Knapp. "Mean," "sneaky," and "cruel" are three terms that are invariably used to describe each.

"Okay," we say, "which of the two characters *most* represents these traits, Hamilton Knapp or Michael Froelich?"

It is Hamilton, of course, which allows us to drop Michael from the list. Among the bureaucrats, the school superintendent is *most* reflective of the narrow-minded ignorance that they all to some degree share, and Julian is more reflective of quiet dignity than is his father.

When we've eliminated some of the minor characters, we're usually left with Julian, Mrs. Olinski, and some or all of the members of the Souls as protagonists, and Hamilton

Knapp, Mrs. Olinski, the district superintendent, and some or all of the members of the Souls as antagonists.

Since we have gone from a large number of choices to a few, we can then list the characteristics of each.

Julian

- Different
- Brave
- Polite
- Wise
- Clever
- Respectful
- Witty
- Caring
- Mature
- Leader

Hamilton Knapp

- Jealous
- Mean
- Aggressive
- Smart
- Leader
- Cunning
- Vindictive

district superintendent

- Pushy
- Mean
- Doesn't listen
- Thinks he's smarter than anyone
- Aggressive
- Jealous

Mrs. Olinski

- Insecure
- Insightful
- Unhappy
- Scared
- Open-minded
- Suspicious

The Souls are harder because they share few traits as individuals besides their loneliness and personal failure at the beginning, and their bonding as friends and their success at the end. Ethan, for example, is unfriendly to Julian at the start of the year, only barely acknowledging him on the bus, but Noah is friendly to anyone who approaches him (although few do). Nadia is uppity and superior to hide her hurt, but neither Noah nor Ethan shares these traits. When we make the kids evaluate the Souls (minus Julian) as individuals, it quickly becomes clear that although each of them may be pushing forward or holding back *an* action, none of them is pushing forward or holding back *the* action. When we go back to *most*, everyone generally agrees that if they had to choose one character who *most* represented the Souls, it would be Julian.

When we're down to Julian and Mrs. Olinski for protagonist and Hamilton Knapp, Mrs. Olinski, and the district superintendent for antagonist, we pair them up and see how each of their conflicts play out. (Mrs. Olinski cannot, of course, be both protagonist and antagonist. That kind of thing only occurs in *Dr. Jekyll and Mr. Hyde*, a book we don't do until fifth grade.)

"If Julian is the protagonist," we say, "and Mrs. Olinski is the antagonist, what action is he pushing forward that she is holding back?"

The answer will usually be that Julian is pushing forward being chosen as a member of the group that goes to the Academic Bowl, and that Mrs. Olinski was holding that action back. In fact, she was toying with the idea of appointing Hamilton Knapp instead of Julian, but ultimately decided that there would be something wrong with that choice.

"So what does that make this book about? About winning an Academic Bowl? Does that seem like the author's intention? That it is important to get the right team together in order to win?"

Hmm. Maybe not.

"What about Mrs. Olinski as protagonist against the district superintendent's antagonist? What is the book about then?"

This is a good matchup, and very close to the heart of the book. Mrs. Olinski does seem to be pushing forward a kind of academic excellence and honesty that the district superintendent, with his pretensions, euphemisms, and buzzwords, is holding back. We have often had an excellent discussion about the importance of combating this sort of academic hypocrisy. We ask the kids what is wrong with the district superintendent's position and what is right about Mrs. Olinski's. What difference does it make if you only make a pretense of being sensitive to others (as the district superintendent does) instead of really trying to put yourself in another's place? The district superintendent's willingness to use the word *cripple* as a weapon against Mrs. Olinski in order to win an argument is telling. Ignorance apparently can be found anywhere, even among those in positions of authority.

But, while Mrs. Olinski's struggle against the academic bureaucracy is a perfectly legitimate interpretation of one of the book's themes, is it *the* theme, the one E. L. Konigsburg considered primary when she first put pen to paper?

To answer that question, we ask the group to go yet again to the concept of *most*. Which contest between which characters reflects the book's themes the *most*? It will usually be pretty clear to the group that the crucial matchup in the book is in fact the one between Julian and Hamilton Knapp, and that the answer to what the book is really about lies there.

We ask the group to take a really good look at Julian and Hamilton. Each is a leader, each is smart, and each, in his own way, is aggressive about advancing his values. The conflict is clear. One builds, the other destroys; one is decent, the other is cruel; one is brave, the other is a coward. With all that, Hamilton Knapp has, at least at the start of the book, the enormous advantage of social acceptance. The pranks he pulls are seen as funny by most of the other students, just as they are in all too many real-world middle school environments. We don't like to think of our children as laughing at cruelty, but the fact is that many do. What the author has done is to provide an antidote, a way in which civility and sensitivity can be made to replace what all too many parents and educators see as an unfortunate but inevitable by-product of adolescence.

That antidote is Julian. Julian exhibits a degree of moral courage and decency unmatched by any other character in the book. Julian never hides. Julian never tries to change himself in order to win favor, nor does he stoop to his rival's methods. Julian has faith in himself. He has time, with all of his own problems, to observe Mrs. Olinski and to notice that she, too, is wounded and needs help. It is Julian who arranges for the Souls to take on the task of restoring her faith in people and ultimately herself.

"Could this then be a book about moral courage?" we ask. "A book that tells us that standing up quietly to cruelty and ignorance will work? There is one character that the author uses specifically to demonstrate that Julian's way will ultimately win out over Hamilton Knapp's. Who is it?"

This question always elicits any number of responses, though most of the kids point to the school administrators because, in their ignorance, they passively contribute to the intolerant atmosphere that Ham Knapp is actively pushing forward. Julian triumphs over these characters, as represented by the state commissioner of education who is moderating the Academic Bowl, when he answers the question about acronyms by citing the words *posh* and *tip*. Posh and tip (being of British origin) are not on the commissioner of education's list of possible responses. The commissioner therefore rules against Julian's answer at first, but eventually it is determined by some offstage aides that posh and tip do, in fact, qualify as acronyms, and the commissioner is forced to reverse his ruling.

The kids often see the commissioner and his staff as totally believable while parents see those characters as excessively broad. Whenever this happens, we ask the parents if they would have felt the same as their kids do now when they were in fourth grade, and, surprisingly, most parents seem to have forgotten how they saw the world back then.

"The commissioner of education is a very good guess," we say, "but unfortunately wrong. Try again."

The various members of the Souls are then suggested (and rejected) as well as Mrs. Draper, Mr. Singh, and even Ginger, the dog.

"Nope. It's Michael Froelich. After the Academic Bowl semifinals, when almost the entire student body of Epiphany Middle School is cheering for the Souls after their victory, Michael Froelich is right out front with them. Why is that important?"

Because he changed sides. Michael Froelich is a follower. He had been Hamilton Knapp's number two, and when he starts cheering for the Souls, it shows that he has left Hamilton for Julian, rejecting ignorance and cruelty as ploys to win popularity. That is how you know that Hamilton Knapp has been defeated.

And so, at its heart, *The View from Saturday* is a book that puts forth the thesis that quiet courage, decency, and intelligence are the best weapons against thoughtlessness, selfishness, and self-absorption. That is why we make a point of discussing it every year.

CHAPTER 12

ONE MORE BOOK FOR PRACTICE

In our fourth-grade groups, after *Animal Farm*, we move from pigs to dogs. *The Call of the Wild* by Jack London is one of the most widely read tales in the English language and another example of an author using an animal story as a cover for something deeper. Unlike the broad and satiric *Animal Farm*, however, *The Call of the Wild* is stark, brutal, and realistic.

The Call of the Wild

This is the story of Buck, an enormous St. Bernard/Shepherd mix, and his journey from pampered and beloved pet on a California farm to ferocious leader of a pack of wolves in the Yukon.

At the opening of the story, Buck is lolling about on Judge Miller's ranch near San Francisco, sometime in the late 1890s. One of the ranch hands, aware that sled dogs are needed in the Klondike to fuel the demand brought on by the gold rush, kidnaps the unsuspecting Buck and sells him to a dealer who ships him off to Seattle. There Buck is alternately fed and beaten (depending on whether he behaves) by a man in a red sweater who expertly wields a club to back up his authority. Buck, who has never known mistreatment, at first fights back, but is soon clever enough to realize that, despite his greater size and strength, the man in the red sweater will defeat him. So, rather than continue to resist, he submits, deciding to wait until the odds turn in his favor.

Before that happens, he is sold and shipped north to be a part of the team that pulls a sled for Perrault and François, who deliver mail for the Canadian government across the frozen wastes of the Klondike. Three other dogs are shipped with him, the sullen and morose Dave, the friendly and gentle Curly, and the wily, vicious Spitz. Soon after they land, Curly is downed in a fight with a husky and ferociously killed by the other dogs. Buck understands that Curly's fate will be his if he is bested in battle.

The team embarks on a journey that will cover hundreds of miles with the experienced Spitz in the lead. Perrault and François are both decent and fair, but do not hesitate to use their whips on dogs who steal food, attack other dogs, or otherwise make trouble. It is only because of Buck's strength and intelligence that he is able to survive in those first days in the wild. Soon, however, he becomes leaner and tougher, adapting to the harsh conditions.

Buck and Spitz become immediate enemies, Spitz understanding that Buck is a threat to his supremacy. Buck knows Spitz will kill him as soon as he gets a chance and that François and Perrault, while favoring him, will not interfere in this primal combat. Finally, the fight comes and Buck, torn and bloody, on the verge of defeat and death, uses superior intelligence and "imagination" (the author's word) to maneuver Spitz into a vulnerable position. Buck makes the most of his advantage and breaks both of his rival's front legs. The hated Spitz is brought down and torn to pieces by the other dogs. Buck takes his place at the head of the team.

At the end of their run, François and Perrault pass out of Buck's life as quickly as they had entered it and a "Scotch half-breed" takes over the team for the return trip. It is grim work for human and animal alike, but the dogs and men work together to survive. When Dave becomes too weak to continue, the men, after first trying to help, are forced to shoot him. Buck understands that, in his new life, there might occasionally be kindness but there will never be mercy.

At the end of the return trip, the team is purchased by Charles, Hal, and Mercedes, three rich people who have come to the Yukon on a lark to prospect for gold. It would be almost impossible to find three people more unsuited to the circumstances. They overpack the sled, weighing it down with nonessentials, and then after it tips over, repack it almost as badly. They have no respect for the harsh country in which they have decided to make a quick fortune and refuse to listen to advice from seasoned hands. They overfeed the dogs at the beginning of the trip, then run out of food for them, so that Buck and the others are soon hungry and weakened.

Finally, after weeks of near starvation, beatings, and abuse, they come to the camp of John Thornton, next to a frozen lake. Thornton warns them that the ice is too thin to take the weight of the sled, but the three insist on crossing anyway. Buck refuses to move. He simply lays there while Hal rains blows upon him. Finally, Thornton tells Hal that if he hits the dog again, he'll kill him. Buck is cut loose and watches as the rest of the team, the sled, and the three prospectors start across the lake. Just as Thornton said, the ice gives way and all are drowned.

Thornton is the kindest and most decent of Buck's owners and Buck loves him. When some men in town bet Thornton that Buck can't haul a sled loaded with a thousand pounds a hundred yards down the road, Buck strains and almost bursts his heart to win the bet.

Still, Buck knows that something is wrong. During his journey from Judge Miller's ranch to Thornton's camp, he has been hearing a call to return to a more primitive life as a hunter in the forests. The call has grown strong, but Buck's love for Thornton keeps him from heeding it. At night he often goes off alone into the woods, but always returns, sometimes the following morning, sometimes days later. During one of these journeys, he makes contact with a wolf, and during another he kills a moose.

Then, one night, while Buck is away, Thornton is killed in an ambush by a marauding pack of Indians. Thornton's death breaks the last hold human civilization has on Buck. He takes his revenge by killing the Indians who murdered Thornton, then escapes permanently into the wild. At the end, he has become the leader of a pack of wolves, content that he has at last found his true nature and his true home.

There isn't a whole lot of doubt in *The Call of the Wild* about who is the protagonist. Although we occasionally get a vote or two for Thornton, every group usually establishes Buck right away. When we ask for traits, however, after "smart" and "strong," there doesn't seem to be anything the group agrees on. Buck's particular traits seem to depend on what part of the book one is talking about.

"Okay," we say, "let's hold off and move on to antagonist."

The choice of antagonist is more difficult still. When we ask for nominations, we usually get just about all of Buck's owners and Spitz.

We point out that the owners are pretty different. If Thornton is the antagonist, it's going to be a far different book than if it's the man in the red sweater. And then if it's Spitz, it would probably be about something different altogether, so we list some traits for all the possible human antagonists, saving Spitz until later.

Judge Miller is usually described as "kind" and "loves Buck," the man in the red sweater is "cruel," "mean," and, significantly, "does his job" and "is fair." François, Perrault, and the Scotsman are also seen as fair and decent masters. The three prospectors come in for the most abuse. "Stupid," "mean," "cruel," and even "deserved to die" regularly make the list. Thornton is just the opposite. "Kind," "gentle," "saves Buck," "loves Buck," and "good master" always make the list.

After that, we list Buck's traits under each of his owners.

Judge Miller

- Lazy
- Ignorant
- Fat
- Happy

Red Sweater

- Cunning
- Afraid
- Patient
- Unhappy

Mailmen

- Thinner
- Fights Spitz
- Leader

Prospectors

- Survives
- Refuses to work

Thornton

- Ferocious
- Loyal
- Performs tricks

Finally, we make a list of Buck's character traits at the beginning of the book and another for the end.

In one of the groups, this is what we got back:

Beginning

- Tame
- Ignorant
- Happy
- Lazy
- Pampered
- Innocent
- Unaware
- Trusting
- Strong

End

- Stronger
- Ambitious
- Smart
- Cunning
- Tough
- Violent
- Leader
- More alive
- Free

"Wow. What's better?" we asked.

To most of the kids, the second list was definitely the more appealing.

"But wait a minute," we said, "at the beginning of the book Buck is this big, furry, friendly, cuddly pet, but by the end he's a killer. Are you trying to say that a killer is more appealing than a big, furry, friendly, cuddly pet?"

No one was trying to say that, but the second list was still somehow more correct.

"Well, you can't have it both ways," we replied. "If the second list is better, then a killer is better."

Eventually, we work the group around to understanding that the second list wasn't necessarily *better*; it was just better for *Buck*.

"Why?" we asked.

"He's not a person," said Megan.

"He's a dog," said Taylor. The competition between Megan and Taylor had grown every bit as ferocious as that between Buck and Spitz. We realized that if we called on one, we immediately had to call on the other.

"He needs to hunt," said Andrew.

The second list, of course, represented Buck's true nature, what he was happiest being. "So if that's true," we went on, "who's the first list better for?"

"Judge Miller."

"Thornton."

"François and Perrault."

"People," said Jordan's mom.

"That's right, it is best for people. So what does that mean people are trying to do to Buck's real nature?"

"Change it," said Megan.

"Change it," said Taylor.

"But just the bad people, right? The man in the red sweater and Charles, Hal, and Mercedes?"

Everyone paused. The truth was that every human was

trying to change Buck's nature, or at least make him deny what his genuine nature was. Even Thornton, the best of the bunch, who let Buck roam free at night, was changing Buck's nature by keeping him from his destiny as a leader in the wild. Buck no more belonged pulling a sled than did Thornton himself.

"Does that mean that the book might be about the same thing no matter who the antagonist is?" we asked.

"Yes," Taylor agreed. "It does."

"It's about the same thing," asserted Megan.

In fact, allegory can be analyzed in much the same fashion as poetry. Once the kids have examined the story, they can think about how it "opens up"—that is, goes from a literal meaning to its allegorical meaning, the underlying theme. Unlike in a poem like "The Road Not Taken," however, where it is possible to pinpoint the transition, in an allegory the theme appears throughout as a subtext. In every episode of *The Call of the Wild,* Buck's relationship with people—and what is similar about his relationships with very different people—is where the deeper meaning of the book can be found.

"So if the book is about the same thing no matter which of the characters is the antagonist, what would that be?"

When even Megan and Taylor couldn't come up with an answer, we said, "Let's do it a different way. What did all the people you listed as antagonists have in common?"

"They were all Buck's owners," said Jordan.

"What's another word for owner?"

"Proprietor," said a dad.

"CEO," said Taylor.

"What's that?" asked Megan.

"Master," said Andrew.

"No," we said. "We're looking for something different. Taylor came closest." Megan looked stricken. "What do you call someone who runs a business that employs other people?"

"Boss?" asked Emma, who hadn't said a thing all year.

"Right! Boss. And if they were all bosses, what does that make the dogs?"

"Workers," said a dad.

"So what you're saying is that on some level this book isn't about a dog in the Yukon but about bosses and workers?"

Maybe.

"Are the bosses in the book the same or different?" we asked.

We got "different" as a first response, as we always do, so we asked how they were different. We divided them up by "good" and "bad." Judge Miller and Thornton were definitely "good" and the three prospectors were definitely "bad," with the man in the red sweater and the mail carriers somewhere in between.

Then we asked, "Is there anything about them that's the same?"

Emma said that Buck had to listen to all of them. Even Thornton, whom he loved, controlled his life.

"But Thornton doesn't *make* Buck do anything, does he?" we asked. "How can he control his life?"

"Buck loves Thornton," said Taylor's dad. "He's loyal."

It is indeed Buck's loyalty and feelings of gratitude that

keep him from leaving Thornton. Even though Buck's actions *appear* to be voluntary, the author seems to be saying that for whatever reason, Buck is denying his own nature.

"So, if *The Call of the Wild* is really about workers and bosses, what is the author saying about that relationship?"

By this time, some of the parents usually understand, but the kids, most of whom have never heard of Jack London, or at least know nothing about him, have no idea. This group was no different.

"You can get a big hint to what's underneath this story if you know something about the author," we said. "Jack London was born in 1876 and became the most popular writer in America, but he only lived to be forty years old. *The Call of the Wild* is probably his most famous book, but he wrote a number of other books that were set in the North. But the most important thing to know in understanding this book is that Jack London was a socialist. Socialists are people who believe that no one should own anything as an individual, but that everyone in society should share. They also believe that the boss/worker relationship is unnatural and that people who actually do the work, like Buck, are usually oppressed by the people they work for."

From there it was easy to discuss how each of the owners, even Thornton, caused Buck to deny his nature, just like, according to London, when people have to work for someone else, it causes them to deny their nature. We went into a little history, too, and talked about how socialism was very popular a hundred years ago when many workers were terribly mistreated. The growth of labor unions was a direct result of these terrible conditions, and the main reason why workers live better lives today is that people like Jack London brought these conditions to the attention of the public by writing about them.

We asked the kids and parents how they felt about this, whether they agreed or disagreed that when people work for other people it forces them to deny their nature.

"I think that's right," said Megan.

"Can you give an example?" we asked.

"School," she replied instantly.

"I disagree," said Taylor, coming to the defense of management. "Some people always need to work for other people."

Emma raised her hand again. "Things were different then," she said. "Maybe it's not as bad to be a worker now."

Many parents agreed with this.

"There was another book published about the same time called *The Jungle*, by a man named Upton Sinclair," we said. "That book was set in the meat-packing plants of Chicago, where the conditions were *horrible* and resulted in a whole set of laws being passed about the way these plants could be run. So why do you think Jack London chose a dog story in the Klondike as *his* setting for a story about workers and bosses?"

Jordan said, "Because people like animals."

"So?" we asked.

"It's like in *Animal Farm*," said Taylor's dad. "Animals are more sympathetic."

We talked for a while about why people will sometimes

have more sympathy for animals than for other people. There is no way to know for sure, but it seems likely that London chose dogs to portray the more sympathetic characters and humans to portray the more villainous characters in order to say that we all share in the exploitation of those who are weaker and more vulnerable.

"But what about Spitz?" we asked. "He certainly wasn't sympathetic."

By that time, most of the kids had figured out that Spitz was in the book to show that workers will try to kill each other when placed in what the author portrayed as an oppressive environment. Dog eat dog.

"So, if it wasn't for the bad conditions, Spitz and Buck would have been friends?" we asked.

No. They never would have been friends. They would have fought anyway.

"Was Jack London wrong, then? Would workers compete with each other—dog eat dog—even if there were no bosses?"

Kids have no trouble agreeing that Jack London might have been wrong, especially in the context of this story, but parents, who have been raised to accept the content of any "great book" find it a bit disconcerting to question a classic.

CHAPTER 13

SOME (ALMOST) FINAL THOUGHTS

We have been running book groups for six years. Our first year of second through fourth grade quickly grew to include fifth. Then, families who had been with us since the beginning didn't want to stop, so, in addition to groups at the library, we now hold meetings for middle schoolers in private homes.

There was no way to know in that very first session of *Mr. Popper's Penguins* that some of those same children would today, in the seventh grade, be discussing the moral implications of military occupation in John Steinbeck's *The Moon Is Down*, or the dynamics of mob rule in Walter van Tilburg Clark's *Ox Bow Incident*. We have gone from teaching these children about literature to having them teach us.

The most important thing that has come out of these discussion groups is that when a child learns that he or she need not simply run through a book and chalk it up as having been read, but rather should delve into what the book means, a great leap occurs. The children make connections to other books or other fields, and develop a context within which to approach everything—from what they see on television to how to stand up to a bully on the school playground. This leap has been reflected in their school-work. More than once, parents have told us that their child's teacher has commented at school conferences on their son's or daughter's increased ability to read, understand, and participate in classroom discussions.

In our book groups, parents and children speak to one another with mutual respect, as equals. Often a child and a parent will take different sides of a question and the room will divide strictly on the basis of argument and not age. In the higher grades, parents and children have become so proficient that if a transcript of a meeting were produced with only first names, it would be impossible to tell the adults from the kids. More than that, because we talk about real issues, the kids come away with insights into their parents (and vice versa) that we have been told spills over into other parts of their relationship.

Critical thinking is not an affectation, but an essential skill, necessary for making one's way in the world. To teach children to become effective and critical readers, these are the rules we go by:

What children read *is* important. The theory, still in vogue, that says that it doesn't matter what your child reads as long as he or she reads *something* is just plain wrong. If anyone tries to convince you otherwise, *don't believe it*. This notion springs from the assumption that kids need success—any success—to bolster their self-esteem, and if they have to struggle a little it might leave them feeling *bad* about themselves. Nothing could be more wrongheaded or insulting to children. Kids' self-esteem comes from the same source as adults' self-esteem: taking on something that seems hard at first and then doing better at it than you ever thought possible. Kids are hip; they know when they're being dumbed down, and no child develops genuine self-esteem from being praised for something he or she didn't work at.

If you start your children off with books that are well-written, whose plots demand attention, with characters drawn with depth and wit, that is the type of reading they will come to enjoy. On the other hand, kids who are exposed to nothing but pop fiction or joke books or superficial biographies of sports heroes will become used to those and are unlikely to move to anything more challenging. During the past five years, we've heard from parents again and again how difficult it has been to get children who have read nothing but pap to focus when the books assigned in class get more complicated.

You wouldn't believe someone who said it didn't matter what your child ate as long as they ate something, and then fed them candy all day. Reading is no different.

Kids enjoy depth. The idea that a boy or girl will only be interested in discussing a book in a superficial way is another misguided assumption. As a result, there has been a trend away from critical analysis and toward personal identification—as in, "I liked this book because the main character has a cat and I have a cat." Not only does this approach require no real thought, children know that it's baloney for any answer to be correct.

The irony is that it is far more fun for kids (and adults) to try and solve the mystery of a book. Kids are capable of a remarkable level of sophistication regardless of their reading level. What they lack is context. Provide that and almost any child will respond. Once they learn *how* to look for clues, even kids who are struggling with the words on the page will surprise you with their insights about character, plot, and even the author's motives.

Have a blueprint for the discussion. In the same way that you would not invite a seven-year-old to a party, hand her a glass of white wine, and tell her to mingle, you cannot hold a discussion with a child the way you would an adult at a dinner party or book group. You have to have an idea of what you want to say, what you want the child to walk away with, and how you are going to get there. You have to be able to identify questions or answers that lead only to dead ends or superficial observations (so that you can steer away from them) and manage the discussion in such a way as to make steady, identifiable progress that the children can follow. It must be like a treasure hunt where the discovery of each clue is a source of excitement, a marker that you are on the right path to the solution, and a spur to search for the next clue. Discussing a book with a child is much more a process than a result.

That being said, no one needs an advanced degree in English literature or forty hours a week of free time to be able to effectively discuss a book with a child. This isn't *Crime and Punishment,* it is *Charlotte's Web.* Children's literature is by definition less subtle and more approachable than adult fiction. The author *wants* the child to get the message, and with a little practice, any parent will pick up the themes right away. Moreover, quality children's literature is every bit as gripping and well-written as adult fiction and just as much fun to talk about.

Group books by theme. It is not difficult to find a number of books that deal with the same issues. For example, part of our third-grade reading list addresses the general theme of whether someone should face a problem or try to escape from it. We use Edward Eager's *Half Magic* about an unhappy family of children who find a magic coin, *The Crazy Mixed-Up Files of Mrs. Basil E. Frankweiler,* and *The Phantom Tollbooth.* In the fourth grade, we deal with issues of authority and conformity. Some of the books we use are *The View from Saturday, The Giver,* and *Animal Farm.* By using this multiple-book approach, we not only build on an idea but allow the kids to contrast styles and rate the author's success at communicating his or her message.

Be patient. While the techniques we're putting forth are meant to be accessible to kids, this will all be new and take a little time. Many kids will tend to have good things to say before they've actually worked up the courage to say them. It is important to engage children early in the process to communicate that you are interested in their opinion.

Show enthusiasm. This is *fun.* If you behave as if this is medicine your children need to take, or that they had better learn to think critically or they won't get into a good college, which means they won't get a good job, which means that their life is effectively over, you're not going to get a whole lot back.

Running our book groups has been one of the most rewarding experiences of our lives. We have been privileged to share in the intellectual growth of not only our daughter and her friends but of many other children in the town in which we live. The best part is that every September, the experience renews itself.

BOOKS FOR SECOND
AND THIRD GRADE

We wanted to include a sampling of books that we think you and your child would enjoy talking about, but as you read through the lists there are some things to bear in mind:

These are *our* lists. We have clearly gravitated toward social themes, but if there is an issue that is of particular interest to your family, such as divorce, peer pressure, or even the death of a loved one, by all means try and find books that explore these as well. If you do choose other issues to explore with your children, try to get a variety of perspectives and compare them using a consistent critical framework.

Nobody can read everything. There are doubtless any number of wonderful and worthwhile books by terrific authors of which we are totally unaware or simply have not read. The object here is not to impose our suggestions but to help parents become more discerning judges of what they recommend to their children.

Lawrence and Nancy Goldstone

There is nothing wrong with "good reads." Just because a book does not necessarily lend itself to critical analysis doesn't mean your child should avoid it. Well-written, carefully plotted stories, such as those in the Harry Potter series or *The Thief Lord* by Cornelia Funke, are completely worthwhile as entertainment and are certainly far superior to television or video games.

We have only listed one or two books by an author. We have chosen those books we feel represent his or her best work for critical discussion. If you think a different book by an author would be better for you and your child, by all means use it.

Here are the books we do in our second- and third-grade book groups. We've covered most of them already.

Second Grade

- *Mr. Popper's Penguins* by Florence and Richard Atwater
- *Babe: The Gallant Pig* by Dick King-Smith
- *Charlotte's Web* by E. B. White
- Poetry
- *Frindle* by Andrew Clements

Third Grade

- *Half Magic* by Edward Eager
- *The Mixed-up Files of Mrs. Basil E. Frankweiler* by E. L. Konigsburg
- *The Phantom Tollbooth* by Norton Juster

▸ *The Enormous Egg* by Oliver Butterworth
▸ *Bull Run* by Paul Fleischman

Half Magic by Edward Eager

Four children find a magic coin on the sidewalk. The catch is that the coin will only grant half of whatever they wish for. Against a backdrop of funny adventures and mishaps, the children learn that a problem doesn't go away unless you face it.

The Enormous Egg by Oliver Butterworth

This tale of a dinosaur that hatches from a chicken's egg is actually a satire that pits Washington, D.C., big politics against homespun New England values. It raises the question as to whether it is possible for our country to have a national character and, if so, what that character should be.

There are lots of alternates that will work as well. Try these:

The Trouble with Jenny's Ear by Oliver Butterworth

Butterworth uses the quiz-show rage of the 1950s to satirize the rise of television and technology, an easy parallel to today's information revolution. But the most potent intellectual tool is still thinking for yourself.

The Cricket in Times Square by George Selden

A country cricket comes to New York City and uses music to save a poor immigrant family's newsstand. Can something as simple as a song affect the way people think, feel, and act?

The Great Turkey Walk by Kathleen Karr

A spoof based loosely on a true episode in our nation's history, where, instead of cattle, enterprising pioneers walked flocks of turkeys from Missouri to Colorado to make a quick buck. An effective demonstration that heroes come in all shapes and sizes and with a variety of character flaws.

Just a Few Words Mr. Lincoln by Jean Fritz

A biography of Abraham Lincoln that stresses the human side of his presidency. A wonderful way to introduce children to moral courage. Don't forget to go over the Gettysburg Address at the end of the book.

The Landry News by Andrew Clements

Like *Frindle*, this story features a bright, slightly rebellious student who helps a teacher recover his enthusiasm for his work by starting a school newspaper. An introduction to First Amendment freedoms and the importance and limitations of free speech and a free press.

Dealing with Dragons by Patricia E. Wrede

This sassy look at princesses in fairy tales turns convention on its head. The heroine wants to do what all the boys do and doesn't want to just marry a prince and live happily—or in her case, unhappily—ever after. Great for discussing gender roles and stereotypes in literature.

The School Mouse by Dick King-Smith

A young mouse learns to read against prevailing mouse wisdom, then saves his family by reading the label on a container of poison. A book that underlines the value of learning and curiosity.

Five Children and It by E. Nesbit

Another magic book about five children who find an ancient Psammead (sand fairy) who grants them wishes. Like *Half Magic,* the wishes go all wrong and the children learn to think carefully about what it is they really want.

BOOKS FOR FOURTH AND FIFTH GRADE

 These are our lists:

Fourth Grade

- *The View from Saturday* by E. L. Konigsburg
- *White Lilacs* by Carolyn Meyer
- *The Giver* by Lois Lowry
- *Animal Farm* by George Orwell
- *The Call of the Wild* by Jack London

Fifth Grade

- *A Wrinkle in Time* by Madeline L'Engle
- *Macario* by B. Traven
- *Lost Horizon* by James Hilton
- *The Strange Case of Dr. Jekyll and Mr. Hyde* by Robert Louis Stevenson
- *The Time Machine* by H. G. Wells

A Wrinkle in Time by Madeline L'Engle

This classic science fiction tale of a girl trying to rescue her father from an interplanetary monster is actually a morality tale with deep spiritual and political undertones. As in *The Giver,* you need to look carefully to decide if you think the author has played fair.

Macario by B. Traven

A fascinating fable about a desperately poor, hardworking Mexican charcoal gatherer who is suddenly granted powers to heal the sick. An excellent vehicle for discussing the true nature of happiness. (Available in *The Night Visitor and Other Stories.*)

The Strange Case of Dr. Jekyll and Mr. Hyde by Robert Louis Stevenson

Stevenson's tale of a kindly but unhappy doctor who takes a potion and turns into a beastly but far happier sociopath. The book is much more even-handed than any of the film versions. Jekyll and Hyde can be contrasted to discuss whether any human traits are, by definition, "good" or "bad," and the nature of fulfillment.

The Time Machine by H. G. Wells

Less of a thriller than is portrayed in popular adaptations, this is actually another book in which man's nature is split, this time between the gentle, childlike Eloi and the industrious, ferocious Morlocks. List the characteristics of both and then discuss which of the two is more appealing as man's "true" nature. An excellent contrast with *Jekyll and Hyde.*

Here are some alternates:

Number the Stars by Lois Lowry

The book details the Nazi occupation of Denmark and a young girl's efforts to escape with her family. Once more, the author creates a powerful, persuasive picture of the evils of dictatorship. Like *The Giver,* carefully examine whether the author has drawn the characters fairly.

The Hound of the Baskervilles by Arthur Conan Doyle

The most famous Holmes tale of them all, *The Hound of the Baskervilles* details the efforts of the great detective to foil the plot to murder Sir Henry Baskerville while using the legend of a huge, ferocious hound to mask the crime. Holmes, a character who illustrates the superior power of intellect, is by far the most popular and well-known figure in literary history.

Among the Hidden by Margaret Peterson Haddix

Set in a totalitarian society that resembles suburban America, this is a book with a very definite political agenda. It is also a useful work to examine the question of bravery and foolhardiness.

A Christmas Carol by Charles Dickens

At only seventy-one pages, this is the perfect vehicle with which to introduce children to the brilliance of Dickens. As is generally the case, the book is superior to even the best film or television adaptations.

Johnny Tremain by Esther Forbes

Set in colonial America on the verge of revolution, this is an excellent example of scrupulously researched historical fiction that presents a point of view with which we agree (at least in the United States). It is an interesting exercise to try and read this book as if you lived in England and see if you feel the same way about it.

Treasure Island by Robert Louis Stevenson

Stevenson's famous pirate yarn is also an interesting study in the qualities of leadership and how different skills are applicable to different societies.

The War of the Worlds by H. G. Wells

Wells's seemingly invincible invaders from Mars done in by bacteria. This is a fine vehicle to discuss the preservation of the world's resources, the interrelationships of living things, and the delicate balance of life. Side discussions on the possibilities of life elsewhere and humans' place in the cosmos are inevitable and valuable.

Twenty Thousand Leagues Under the Sea by Jules Verne

Captain Nemo and his submarine, the *Nautilus,* wreak havoc on the open seas, destroying shipping to halt the spread of slavery. An outstanding book to introduce the question of whether the ends justify the means.

The Secret Garden by Frances Hodgson Burnett

A look at spiritual healing before Freud. When Mary's parents succumb to a cholera epidemic in India, the unhappy child is sent to the country estate of her uncle in Yorkshire, England. There she finds her uncle and cousin Colin grieving over the accidental death of her aunt. The cure for all three lies in a locked garden. When a spiritual trauma masquerades as physical ailment, what is the best way to effect a cure?

ACKNOWLEDGMENTS

There are a number of people at the Westport Public Library who helped make our book groups a success. The director, Maxine Bleiweis, has been unfailingly supportive of the program. The entire staff of the Children's Department from Kitty on down, has manned the telephones during the land rush of registration, always made sure we had a room and fielded innumerable queries from curious parents. Special thanks go to Candace, who arranges the schedule, and Lynne, Kris, and Annie who do most of the heavy lifting. Faith Taylor, president ex officio of the Friends Association, gave us our start and Mimi Greenlee picked up when she took over the job.

This book would not have been possible without Jed Mattes. Jed passed away in August 2003, but it was his vision and energy in seeing the possibilities for this idea that both got the book off the ground and found it the right home. Jed's associate Fred Morris was also unstintingly generous with his time and energy during Jed's illness.

Our current agent, Henry Dunow, has been a prince. After Jed's death, we never thought we would find someone who could match Jed's enthusiasm, care, professionalism, good humor, and intelligence. We were wrong.

Speaking of enthusiasm, care, professionalism, good humor, and intelligence, our editor, Ileene Smith, has overwhelmed us. We have never before encountered an editor who was so personally involved with her books, nor one so willing to work cooperatively with an author. Her assistants, first Robin Rolewicz and now Luke Epplin, have always been helpful and friendly, even in response to some incredibly stupid questions.

We dedicated this book to the parents and kids in our groups, but we would also like to say how very much they have given to us. We have met any number of extraordinarily committed, generous, and questing parents, who were matched by equally eager, vibrant, and curious children. Seeing their faces during the discussions has been one of the most treasured experiences of our lives.

Finally, there is our daughter Emily. She both inspired us to start the groups and has sustained us in the process. Her own reading has been our greatest reward.

ABOUT THE AUTHORS

Lawrence and Nancy Goldstone have written several well-received memoirs on reading and book collecting as well as narrative history and fiction. For the past six years they have run a highly successful series of parent-child book clubs at their local public library in Connecticut. The Goldstones live with their daughter Emily, and their beagle, Darwin.

ABOUT THE TYPE

This book was set in Sabon, a typeface designed by the well-known German typographer Jan Tschichold (1902–74). Sabon's design is based upon the original letter forms of Claude Garamond and was created specifically to be used for three sources: foundry type for hand composition, Linotype, and Monotype. Tschichold named his typeface for the famous Frankfurt typefounder Jacques Sabon, who died in 1580.